The Lamplighters
of the Phoenix Park

The Lamplighters of the Phoenix Park

A UNIQUE HISTORY OF ONE OF
IRELAND'S MOST FAMOUS PLACES

DONAL FALLON

WITH JAMES AND FRANK FLANAGAN

HACHETTE
BOOKS
IRELAND

First published in Ireland in 2023 by
HACHETTE BOOKS IRELAND

1

Cataloguing in Publication Data is available from the British Library

ISBN 9781399722810

Typeset in 10.5pt Baskerville
Book design and typesetting by Anú Design, Tara

Printed and bound in Italy by
L.E.G.O. S.p.A.

Hachette Books Ireland policy is to use papers that are natural, renewable and
recyclable products and made from wood grown in sustainable forests. The logging
and manufacturing processes are expected to conform to the environmental
regulations of the country of origin.

Hachette Books Ireland
8 Castlecourt Centre
Castleknock
Dublin 15, Ireland

A division of Hachette UK Ltd
Carmelite House, 50 Victoria Embankment, London EC4Y 0DZ

www.hachettebooksireland.ie

To the memory of
Nicholas and Tom Flanagan,
Phoenix Park lamplighters.

The Phoenix Park is the greatest and most abiding monument of that extraordinary revival and extension of the Irish capital which followed the Restoration, and which in the space of a few years transformed Dublin from a mediaeval city into a modern metropolis.

C. Litton Falkiner,
Proceedings of the Royal Irish Academy, 1903

Luke Fallon.

We can visualise the cavalry charges down the Fifteen Acres, the old armoured cars of the Tans and the Wiltshires, the polo horses of old, the many generations of deer culled down to fifty during the War ... Amidst these we carry on the tradition of the old lamplighters and we love it.

Frank Flanagan, Phoenix Park lamplighter

Luke Fallon.

Contents

James Flanagan attending to a gas lamp in the Phoenix Park (Luke Fallon).

Introduction

James Flanagan was standing at the top of a ladder in the Phoenix Park, attending to the timer of a gas lamp near to the Hole in the Wall public house. The weather was turning, and the latter seemed more and more appealing. Below, wiping raindrops from the front of his camera, my brother snapped one of a series of images for this book. 'Is that an old film camera?', James asks down to Luke. 'You don't see many of them now.' There's a moment of laughter as Luke replies, 'I don't know, you're the one fixing a Victorian gas lamp!' Across Europe and beyond, such lamps are quickly fading from the streetscape. It's a very different fortune from the resurrection of the film camera.

2022 was an interesting time to undertake a study like this, against the backdrop of the Russian invasion of Ukraine. In Berlin, a city which has a longstanding love affair with gas lamp lighting, it was reported that 'what was once a quirky curiosity easily afforded by the capital of a wealthy country is now a problem for city authorities as Germany prepares for a future without the Russian gas that has fuelled its industry for decades'.[1] A visitor to Berlin will encounter the Gaslaternen-Freilichtmuseum in Tiergarten, where dozens of gas

---

1 Euronews, 22 August 2022.

lanterns from across Europe are displayed, including one from the Phoenix Park.

The distinctive glow of gas lamps can still be seen in the Charlottenburg area of the city especially. Nearly half of the world's gas lamps today are to be found on the streets of Berlin, but rising costs, political uncertainty around the provision of gas and environmental concerns all seem to be working against the lights there. Bertold Kujath, a campaigner for the preservation of the gas lamps, has insisted that 'Berlin's gas street lighting is a glowing testimonial to an outstanding era of style and industry. We cannot allow globally unique cultural heritage to be thrown on the scrapheap.'[2] Since making that appeal a decade ago, almost twenty thousand gas lamps have been replaced in the city.

Berlin's relationship with gas lamps raises interesting questions around authenticity. The World Monuments Fund placed Berlin's gas lamps on its 2014 list of endangered cultural resources, but this only led to discussion over what exactly should be preserved, the lamps themselves or the gas lighting? Several thousand gas lights have now been retrofitted with LED lighting, specifically designed to give off the same unique colour as gas lighting. If there is 'no perceivable difference in brightness, colour or form', what does this mean? For some residents, historians and others, a gas lamp without gas does not constitute genuine heritage.[3]

Beyond the streets of the *Hauptstadt*, as Berliners affectionately know their capital, there are other European cities that bring gas lamps to mind. Reversing trends, Prague has sought to increase the presence of gas lamp lighting on its streetscape in recent times. In London, a pioneering city in the development of the technology, more than 250 gas lamps survive in the Westminster area. Having withstood not only technological change but the Blitz too, these lamps are one of few constants in an ever-changing city. London's fog has been described

2 *The Independent*, 29 September 2012. 3 Sandy Isenstadt, Margaret Maile Petty and Dietrich Neumann, *Cities of Light: Two Centuries of Urban Illumination* (London, 2014), 71.

The wall separating Blackhorse Avenue and the Phoenix Park (Luke Fallon).

as 'the greatest character of nineteenth-century fiction', but her gaslit Westminster streets are part of her unique atmosphere too.[4]

Yet few places are as synonymous with this historic lighting as Dublin's largest park. Writing about a drive through the park in the 1970s, a journalist with the *Evening Herald* described the experience as 'Sherlock Holmesian. The gas lamps swelled with yellow softness as we approached them and the fog coiled in great serpent-like undulations amid the trees.'[5] The best place to see these lights is on Chesterfield Avenue, the main artery of the Phoenix Park, which brings the visitor from Parkgate Street to the Castleknock Gate, at just over 3.7 miles. Now free of cars since the pandemic led to a rethinking of the park and access, both sides of the road are lit in a beautiful, soft yellow glow each evening. Some people even come to watch them flicker on, in slow procession as the timers do their jobs.

---

4 For an interesting study of London lighting past, present and future, see Julian Hunt (ed.), *London's Environment: Prospects for a Sustainable World City* (London, 2005). 5 *Evening Herald*, 28 October 1976.

The Flanagan family have a connection to the Phoenix Park which stretches back even before the introduction of these lamps into the park. Their family have worked in the stately homes that dot the park, such as the Viceregal Lodge; have laboured throughout the park and its environs; and have been at the heart of the community of Blackhorse Lane and Blackhorse Avenue, the community that exists outside the park walls. The Phoenix Park assassinations of 1882, the repairing of the Wellington Testimonial – a towering tribute to the Duke of Wellington that is visible from far beyond the park – the glory days of the Phoenix Park racecourse and other events and places are all recalled within their collective family memory. Going about their work of illuminating the park, they have met presidents, beginning with Douglas Hyde, and have encountered many others for whom the Phoenix Park is a place of work and residence, like U.S ambassadors. What perhaps began in my mind as an oral history of a single family and their labour instead became something much broader. Is it possible to tell the story of the Phoenix Park, an integral part of the story of the capital, through the prism of the Flanagan family and the events that have occurred in the century and a half that the family has worked in and around it?

In Dublin, it is not entirely uncommon that families remain within a tradition. When the iconic Dublin City Fruit and Vegetable Market opened for business in 1892 just off bustling Capel Street, one of the first traders was Kate Leonard. Today, Jackie Leonard & Sons continues in that same family tradition, just around the corner from the redbrick markets building on Cuckoo Lane. Fanagans Funeral Directors began life in 1819, and remains in the same family today, while Nichols is another name in the same industry stretching back even further in the hands of one family (and even warranting passing mention in *Ulysses*).[6] There are families of three generations

6 Paula Howard and Gus Nichols, *Past Nichols the Undertakers* (Dublin, 2014)

Frank Flanagan photographed in the Phoenix Park, April 2023 (Luke Fallon).

and occasionally more within the emergency services, inheriting the nicknames of loved ones from different times. What is unique about the Flanagan family is that the skillset itself, unlike burying the dead or fighting the fires of the city, has been so radically altered by a changing world. Those who followed grandfathers into cooperage behind the walls of the St James's Gate brewery were considered amongst the aristocracy of labour, until changing practices relegated their skillsets. The Flanagans are the last outpost of something that was once commonplace, and now exists exclusively within the walled Phoenix Park.

At ninety-two, Frank Flanagan's memory stretches back clearly to the Emergency (as the Irish State knew the Second World War), a transformative time for the Phoenix Park. He describes a place that is unimaginable today, as the park shifted from a centre of recreation to one of wartime resources. While the pandemic may have closed Chesterfield Avenue to car-parking, Frank can remember in vivid detail the days of the 'New Bog Road', when mountains of stacked materials lined both sides of the avenue, in the hope of providing fuel and heat to a wartime nation, one which was not entangled in the conflict itself but still felt its repercussions sharply. The name was not official, but it was difficult for anyone who lived through the war years to imagine Chesterfield Avenue ever returning to its former glory. James Flanagan, the younger sibling at 79, has a particular interest in the technology around their family tradition. He talks of the latest developments in gas lighting, and the contemporary manufacturers in places like Germany and India, in a way some talk about the latest in computers or communications devices. Frank illuminated the past and the family journey, but James made me think about these lights not as a Victorian curiosity, but something which adds to the living feeling of an urban or park environment.

There are other voices within these pages too. John McCullen, former chief park superintendent, who radically transformed the perception of the Phoenix Park in the 1980s. Refusing to allow it to become little more than a road for suburban traffic, McCullen focused media attention onto the possibilities of the Phoenix Park, believing the park could shine as a resource for those who visited it. He has also published the most ambitious history of the Phoenix Park to date, and is working on its sequel. We meet Margaret Gormley (chief park superintendent) and Paul McDonnell (park superintendent), both central to the operating of the park today, who have brought it to leading international recognition, winning the prestigious Gold International Large Parks Award in 2018. We also meet Ronan Clarke and John Kelly, sons-in-law to the Flanagan brothers, who could never have imagined that they would become a part of a family story stretching back to Victorian times. They married into a tradition, and have fully embraced it. With grandsons Matthew Flanagan and Conor Clarke assisting too in the lighting and maintenance of the lamps, this story now stretches over five generations of an extended family.

Like any city, Dublin has had a complex relationship with its parks. Some remained private, residents-only spaces into the late Victorian age, like St Stephen's Green, landscaped and gifted to the people of the city by Arthur Edward Guinness, Lord Ardilaun, only in the 1880s. Before that, it had been in and out of public access. In 1635, Dublin Corporation resolved that 'Hoggen Greene, St Stephens Greene and Oxmanton Greene … may bee wholie kept for the use of the citizens and others, to walke and take the open aire, by reason this cittie is at present groweing very populous'.[7] Having fallen into disrepair, it was locked to the public, remaining so until Ardilaun's great gesture. His statue sits in the park today, looking towards the family empire and the brewery in the heart of the Liberties. Prior to that date, those who lived around the park could enjoy it at their own leisure, renting its keys. Its opening coincided with a moment of such reforms elsewhere, a time that Harriet Jordan, an authority on the history of public parks, describes as 'the height of the parks movement', against the backdrop of 'a fashion for magnificent philanthropic gestures [where] the gift of a park from a wealthy citizen became a common occurrence'.[8]

Merrion Square Park remained a privately controlled space until 1974, when the press reported that 'hundreds of children cheered when, for the first time in 200 years, the padlocks were removed from

---

7 Royal Irish Academy, 'The Architecture of Recreation and Public Resort', in *Art and Architecture of Ireland, Volume IV: Architecture 1600–2000* (Dublin, 2015), 475–506. **8** Harriet Jordan, 'Public Parks, 1885–1914', *Garden History* (Volume 22, Number 1), 85–113, at 85.

the gates of [the park] yesterday'.[9] Long before either of these spaces were given over to public use, the Phoenix Park was familiar territory to all social classes in the city. Its opening to the public, in 1745, came against the backdrop of a changing and expanding city. A Dublin that would come to consider herself the second city of the empire project (other cities would contest the title), though which was also a city of real tensions in class and culture. By the end of that same century, the Phoenix Park would be hosting its first labour demonstrations.[10]

The Phoenix Park holds a special place in the collective memory and identity of the city. We find it, again and again, within the collected works of James Joyce. It touched on several of Joyce's obsessions, ranging from the village of Chapelizod to the Fenian movement. We find it in the poetry of Thomas Kinsella, who grew up just across the Liffey in The Ranch, an area of redbrick housing on the border of Ballyfermot and Inchicore. There, the streets carried the names Phoenix Street and Park Street.[11] The park fascinated Kinsella, as it did Joyce before him. Other poets, like Paula Meehan, have been drawn to it too. In 'The Pattern', Meehan remembers her own mother:

> *There's a photo of her taken in the Phoenix Park*
> *alone on a bench surrounded by roses*
> *as if she had been born to formal gardens.*[12]

Is there a family photo album, from one end of Dublin to the other, without the Phoenix Park somewhere within it?

Beyond literature, the park holds special meaning to many different people. In the sporting arena, it is the birthplace of association football in the city and still its beating heart. Located near to the city, but

---

9 Donal Fallon, '1970s Protests Open Merrion Square Park to the Public', Come Here To Me!, 2 September 2013. Available at: https://comeheretome.com/2013/09/23/1970s-protests-to-open-merrion-square-park-to-the-public/ **10** A.J. Nowlan, 'Phoenix Park Public Meetings', *Dublin Historical Record* (Volume 14, Number 4), 102–13. **11** Thomas Kinsella, *A Dublin Documentary* (Dublin, 2006), 63. **12** Paula Meehan, *The Man who was Marked by Winter* (Dublin, 1991), 19.

also providing plenty of green space, it was a natural draw for anyone seeking to develop the game. If soccer was our 'garrison game' of choice, it's worth noting that migrants from Pakistan, India and other places know the Phoenix Park fondly as the home of cricket in the capital. Cricket may have felt like a colonial legacy in the landscape of the Phoenix Park, but it has won new adherents from these communities and from new Irish players. Today, the Phoenix Cricket Club fields six men's teams and two women's teams. In addition, children learn to cycle there, or make memories in the zoo which will last a lifetime. And not just childhood memories for the children of the capital, but for the thousands who make the pilgrimage to Dublin Zoo every year. For others, the park will always conjure images of standing amongst hundreds of thousands of people, the generation of the 'Pope's Children'. And undoubtedly the Phoenix Park took on new meaning for many in the pandemic, when it offered escapism and recreation.

To John Harvey, the English travel writer and author of one of the great guidebooks to Dublin in the late 1940s, the Phoenix Park was nothing less than 'the most splendid park in Europe in immediate adjacency to a capital'.[13] And while tens of thousands of visitors to the city will pass through it each year, encouraged by Harvey's successors, it is the unique place of the park in the lives of those who live around it that has made it such an intriguing subject for a study such as this.

The park has its contradictions. 'Those who relish examples of the Irish bull,' Maurice Craig noted, 'may find them here.' Of all the entrances, 'it is the one without a gate which is called Parkgate. Similarly, the largest of the open spaces is ludicrously known as The Fifteen Acres, containing as it does over ten times that area.'[14] There are other things about it too that people obsess over, like the curious names of its lakes (how does a lake in a Dublin park become known

---

13 John Harvey, *Dublin: A Study in Environment* (London, 1949), 69–70. 14 Maurice Craig, *Dublin 1660–1860* (Dublin, 1969), 14.

'Phoenix Park' detail as it appears on some lamps in the park (Luke Fallon).

as Machine Lake?), and the exact location of the cross marking the 1882 Phoenix Park assassinations. There is little agreement on just when the cross, explored later, was placed there. Many have stories of the Phoenix Park too, some apocryphal and others the stuff of long-standing local lore. As we shall hear later from Frank Flanagan, the Phoenix Park has its fair share of ghost tales.

This book is about a familiar place, which on one level belongs to us all but which is also a place of lesser-known tales and particularly strong connections. It is difficult to imagine the Phoenix Park without the Flanagan family, who lend to it a core part of its atmosphere. Go and see those gas lamps for yourself, as day gives way to darkness on Chesterfield Avenue.

A Phoenix Park Timeline

By no means a complete timeline of the Phoenix Park, this is intended to give the reader a sense of the timeline at the heart of this story. Many of these events and places are mentioned throughout the work.

1662	Creation of the Phoenix Park as a royal deer park, following the return of James Butler, Duke of Ormond, to Ireland.
1728	Construction of Mountjoy House, today home to the Ordnance Survey of Ireland. Mountjoy House once served as a home to the mounted escort of the lord lieutenant of Ireland.
1735	Construction of the Magazine Fort on St Thomas's Hill, just off the Military Road. The fort was raided at the commencement of the 1916 Easter Rising, and again in December 1939.
1745	The opening of the Phoenix Park to the public by Philip Dormer Stanhope, 4th Earl of Chesterfield.
1751	The construction of Nathaniel Clements's home. In time, this park ranger's lodge would become the Viceregal Lodge, and later Áras an Uachtaráin.
1817	Foundation stone laid for the Wellington Testimonial, honouring Arthur Wellesley, 1st Duke of Wellington.
1830	Foundation of the Phoenix Cricket Club, the oldest cricket club in Ireland. Its founder was John Parnell, father of Charles Stewart Parnell.

1831	The Zoological Society of Ireland succeeds in opening Dublin Zoo. In its infancy, the zoo 'rented an elephant and rhinoceros for the summer months'.[1] It would become a world-class institution, famous for its lions which were first bred in 1857.
1859	The Hibernian Gas Light Company successfully introduces gas to the Phoenix Park.
1878	Unveiling of John Henry Foley's statue of Field Marshal Hugh Gough. The unveiling was the earliest childhood memory of Winston Churchill, whose family were working within the Phoenix Park.
1882	The deaths of Lord Frederick Cavendish (chief secretary for Ireland) and Thomas Henry Burke (permanent under-secretary) at the hands of the Invincibles, an assassination team within the Fenian movement.
1890	Nicholas Flanagan and his brothers begin a family tradition of lighting the Phoenix Park gas lamps.
1890	Bohemian Football Club established at a meeting in the Gate Lodge adjacent to the North Circular Road. Members of the Hibernian Military School, located in the park, were centrally important to the formation of the club.
1916	The Easter Rising begins in Dublin with the raiding of the Magazine Fort.

---

1   Dublin Zoo, 'A Summary History', https://www.dublinzoo.ie/dublin-zoo-history/

1919	Failed assassination attempt on the lord lieutenant of Ireland, Sir John French, at Ashtown beside the Phoenix Park.
1929	The first Irish International Grand Prix is held in the Phoenix Park, on a 4.25 mile circuit. The victor is Boris Ivanowski, a former officer in the Russian army, who claimed the inaugural prize in an Alfa Romeo.
1932	The Eucharistic Congress is held in Dublin from 22 to 26 June. The world-famous tenor Count John McCormack sings in the Phoenix Park. It's estimated that more than a fifth of the population of Ireland attended mass in the park.
1938	Douglas Hyde (Dubhghlas de hÍde) becomes the first President of Ireland. He will reside in the former Viceregal Lodge, before retiring to the former residence of the secretary to the lord lieutenant, now known as Ratra House.
1939–45	In Ireland, the Second World War was known as the Emergency. In a transformative time for the park, Chesterfield Avenue becomes the 'New Bog Road', stacked high with turf.
1979	First Irish visit by a pope. More than a million people attend mass celebrated by Pope John Paul II. At 116 feet tall, the purpose-built cross for this event remains one of the Phoenix Park's most recognisable symbols. It is the work of Scott Tallon Walker Architects.

1988	A major restoration, refurbishment and expansion of the Phoenix Park gas lamps is carried out under the stewardship of John McCullen, chief park superintendent.
2018	Phoenix Park wins a prestigious Gold International Large Parks Award. The awards recognise the quality of parks internationally. Along with the Phoenix Park, the only other winner of a gold award is Centennial Park, in Sydney, Australia.
2018	Pope Francis celebrates mass in the Phoenix Park. Office of Public Works figures suggest an official attendance of just under 152,000.
2020	Covid-19 pandemic brings radical changes to the Phoenix Park, including the closure of Chesterfield Avenue to parking.

Luke Fallon

The Lamplighter

Here's to the leisured side of life,
Remote from traffic, free from strife
A cul-de-sac, a sanctuary
Where old quaint customs creep to die
And only ancient memories stir
At evening comes the lamplighter:
With measured steps, without a sound,
He treads the unalterable round.
Soundlessly touching one by one
The waiting posts that stand to take
The faint blue bubbles in his wake;
And when the night begins to wane
He comes to take them back again
Before the chilly dawn can blight
The delicate frail buds of light.

Seumas O'Sullivan, from
The Lamplighter and Other Poems (1929)

James Malton's view from Capel Street shows a man on a ladder attending to the lamps on the bridge (Library of Congress).

CHAPTER ONE

From Dark Nights to Bright Lights

In the medieval community, all connections with the surrounding world were thoroughly severed after sunset. The city gates which had been opened at sunrise were closed and the individual houses shut tight – their doors locked, their windows shuttered. The town as a whole, as well as the individual houses, prepared for the night not unlike a ship that prepares for a storm ... The period between sunset and sunrise was called by the same name that in present time is reserved for situations of civil unrest: Curfew.[1]

---

1 Wolfgang Schievelbusch, 'The Policing of Street Lighting', *Yale French Studies* (Number 73, 1987), 61–71, at 61.

Original lamp iron on Dublin's Pembroke Street. In a time before gas or electricity, such lamps in railings were once commonplace (Luke Fallon).

When I first read these words by Wolfgang Schievelbusch, a German historian, they transformed how I thought about the Dublin of the past. Though Schievelbusch hails from Berlin, his statement rings true of all societies.

It's fascinating to imagine the Dublin of the past not only as a smaller place than the one we know, but the day itself as something more condensed too. When darkness came, life – at least for most inhabitants – wound down. For some with ulterior motives, darkness brought opportunity. For the crook, perhaps the day began at darkness. The dark, in any urban setting, could bring about a 'second city – with its own geography and its own set of citizens'.[2]

The story of public lighting in Dublin begins with the 1616 Candlelight Law, when an order was made that 'every fifth house in

2 Tim Edensor, 'Introduction to Geographies of Darkness', *Cultural Geographies* (Volume 22, Number 4), 559–65, at 561.

A lamp at the entrance to St. Stephen's Church, Mount Street Upper c. 1960–1980 (Courtesy of National Library of Ireland).

the city and suburbs should have lantern and candlelight set forth from six o'clock to nine on every dark night, from All Hallowmas to Candlemas, and a fortnight after'.[3] By contrast, London's mayor, Sir Henry Barton, had made a similar decree as early as 1416. The cry of the London watchman to 'hang out your lights' became one of the familiar sounds of that great metropolis.

Dublin's authorities, conscious of 'many mischiefes and inconveniences in the streets in the darke nights', would issue further directives on how candlelight should be utilised in the late seventeenth century, and by 1697 the city had appointed 'Michael Cole, Merchant' with the task of public lighting by contract. Cole's successors succeeded in greatly extending public lighting, with lamps fixed on Dublin's bridges. By the end of the eighteenth century, lamps were being incorporated into railings across the city – with as many as ten thousand estimated – but the kind of light provided remained too weak to offer much in the line of either illumination or security.

Tallow candles, produced from animal fats, may not have provided any great sense of lighting, but they were enough to allow for the beginnings of a night-time world and economy if used effectively. In the world of theatre, for example, it has been noted that 'large rings or hoops of these would have hung above the stage; and may have been raised or lowered, depending on the demands of the scene. Other candles were fitted into wall-brackets spaced throughout the auditorium.'[4] Beeswax candles were significantly brighter, but more expensive.

We get a snapshot of the eighteenth century in James Malton's 1790s views of the city. Malton's twenty-five plates, contained within *A Picturesque and Descriptive View of the City of Dublin*, are renderings of a city that focus on its magnificent architecture and views, but which sometimes reveal a lot more on closer inspection. In his 'View

---

3 John Thomas Gilbert, *Calendar of Ancient Records of Dublin* (Dublin, 1892), ix. 4 Gladys L.H. Clark and John C. Greene, *The Dublin Stage, 1720–1745* (Dublin, 1993), 59.

'A Peep at the Gas Lights.' This 1809 print demonstrates an early example of gas lighting in London (The Metropolitan Museum of Art).

from Capel Street, Looking over Essex Bridge', we see poverty in the form of a shoeless beggar asking for assistance, cap in hand. We see public buildings, like the Royal Exchange, now City Hall. We see the military presence in Dublin, with soldiers on horseback. And there, on the Essex Bridge (now Grattan Bridge) we see the lamplighter, going about his task.

As the eighteenth century gave way to the nineteenth, other potential forms of lighting were becoming clear. Our cities came to owe much to William Murdoch, Scottish inventor, mechanical engineer and chemist. Through his work with steam engines, Murdoch came to the conclusion that heated coal developed a flammable gas, and that this could be passed through pipes and torched elsewhere. Other early pioneers in the area included the Rev. John Clayton, who discovered coal gas accidentally and who 'entertained the members of the Royal Society in London with an account of how he had burned a few lumps

Sarah Bridge with lamps on the Liffey, from the Brocas sketchbook (Courtesy of National Library of Ireland).

of the black stuff, released "the spirit of coal", captured it in animal bladders and, to the great amusement of his friends, set it alight'.[5]

By no means alone in experimenting with gas lighting then, the practically minded Murdoch nonetheless had the most significant impact on the lighting of British cities. His contemporary Philippe le Bon would simultaneously bring gas lighting to Paris. Murdoch's successes, such as illuminating the Philips and Lee cotton mill in Manchester in 1805, played no small role in the industrial revolution which would unfold on our neighbouring island. In cities where streets had not even been paved before, the new age of light accelerated progress. Now, 'illuminating gas, made from large quantities of bituminous coal and carried through miles of pipe to thousands of private and public lamps, transformed the dark, sleeping cities into islands of light and activity'.[6]

---

5 *The Guardian*, 31 October 2009. 6 Frederick Moore Binder, 'Gas Light', *Pennsylvania History: A Journal of Mid-Atlantic Studies* (Volume 22, Number 4), 359–73, at 359.

THE LAMPLIGHTERS OF THE PHOENIX PARK

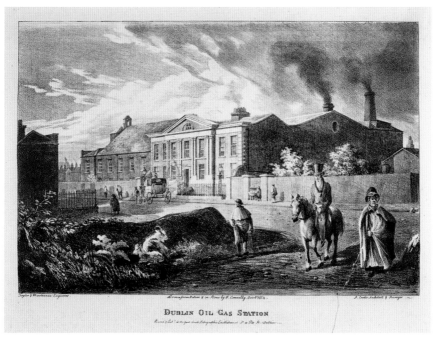

DUBLIN OIL GAS STATION

The Hibernian Gas Light Company premises on Great Brunswick Street. This exterior remains a feature of the streetscape today (Science Museum Group).

Early use of gas in Irish cities was experimental, and often irregular. Readers of one Dublin newspaper were informed in March 1819 for example that the Crow Street Theatre in Temple Bar 'was lit for the first time with gas on Saturday night. The effect was extremely beautiful.'[7] Public gas lighting followed in both Belfast and Dublin in the 1820s, with the creation of the Dublin Coal Gas Company in the capital marking the arrival of the first of several companies in the decade. The Hibernian Gas Light Company built its premises at Great Brunswick Street, now Pearse Street. The artist John Connolly, more familiar for scenic views of Killarney, depicted it in a lithograph that shows the peculiar contrast of the old world and the new, with the poverty of earlier times alongside this radical new advancement.

---

7 John C. Greene, *Theatre in Dublin, 1745–1820: A Calendar of Performances* (Dublin, 2011), 4379.

Stories abound of these early pioneering gas companies and greedy behaviour. Colum McCabe, general manager of the Dublin Gas Company in the 1980s and a committed historian of the development of the industry, wrote of how:

> The three original gas companies operated in competition with one another and laid mains alongside each other on the same streets. Stories were told of foremen being given a bonus for quietly connecting a customer of their own company to the gas main of a rival concern, thus ensuring that their own company got the revenue, while the rival undertaking supplied the gas![8]

In time, a more unified approach led to the emergence of gas street lighting from September 1825, and on principal streets, thousands of old streetlamps would be discarded in the weeks and months that followed. As historian David Dickson notes in his overview of the emergence of Irish cities, this put Dublin 'ahead of most big cities outside Britain', with similar taking place in Cork, Waterford and other large Irish urban centres: 'Where once walls and toll-gates had declared the boundaries of cities, now the nocturnal divide was between the darkness of the *banlieue* and the amply lit city sidewalks. And it was largely English capital as well as English science that drove this revolution.'[9] Every great metropolis took its own approach, but nothing could match New York City for a unique approach to when the streets could be left without lighting:

New York's first streetlamps had been oil lanterns hung from wooden standards; they were replaced in 1827 by cast-iron standards and gas jets. Service to the lamps was supplied by the New York Gas Light Company, and they were not required to be lighted on moonlit nights.[10]

---

8 Colum McCabe, 'History of the Town Gas Industry in Ireland 1823–1980', *Dublin Historical Record* (Volume 45, Number 1), 28–40, at 34. 9 David Dickson, *The First Irish Cities: An Eighteenth-Century Transformation* (Yale, 2021), 235. 10 Mimi Sherman, 'A Look at Nineteenth-Century Lighting: Lighting Devices from the Merchant's House Museum', *APT Bulletin: The Journal of Preservation Technology* (Volume 31, Number 1), 37–43, at 41.

The Turner foundry stamp is still visible on some lamp standards within the Phoenix Park (Luke Fallon).

It would be another three decades from the introduction of gas street lighting in the capital before the Hibernian Gas Light Company succeeded in introducing gas to the Phoenix Park in 1859. Some of the oldest lamp standards in the park still carry the name of Turner foundry, for example those moved in recent times to the entrance of Áras an Uachtaráin. Richard Turner was the leading iron-founder owner of his day, working from an impressive premises at Hammersmith Works in Ballsbridge, later the home of building firm G&T Crampton. The work of the Turner firm is still visible across the city, as they were also the most significant glasshouse designers of the Victorian period in Dublin. From glasshouses in the Botanic Gardens to gas lamps in the Phoenix Park, these are nineteenth-century impacts on the build landscape that remain iconic features.

By the 1880s, electric street lighting had arrived in Dublin. As had been the case with gas lighting, this was initially carried out by private companies, such as the Dublin Electric Light Company, which built a humble generating station in Schoolhouse Lane, off Kildare Street, in 1880. Given permission by the corporation to begin experimenting with lighting streets in their locale, including Nassau Street and St Stephen's Green, it was quickly apparent that the mistakes of the past would not be repeated when it came to ownership and authority. Municipal bodies across Britain and Ireland largely decided to undertake electricity supply themselves, and the Dublin Corporation Electricity Department established itself on Fleet Street in 1893. In those earliest days, electric street lighting lit up O'Connell Street, Grafton Street, St Stephen's Green, Capel Street, Mary Street, Henry Street, D'Olier Street, Cork Hill, Dame Street, College Green and Parliament Street.[11] The issue of how to light the streets of the capital, and other similar issues, was made more difficult by the presence of townships. Rathmines, Pembroke and other areas had essentially gone their own way in the second half of the nineteenth century, becoming in effect their own self-sufficient suburban entities, which created a variety of headaches when it came to issues such as water supply and electricity. In the early years of the twentieth century, an ESB history notes:

An 'Electricity Showroom' was opened at 39 Grafton Street in response to criticism that the Electricity Department of the Corporation lacked selling expertise. This showroom was fully equipped to demonstrate the range of home comforts which could be achieved through electricity. By the early and mid 1920s, no house was considered modern unless it had electric light but the public were only beginning to realise the advantages of using electricity for other purposes around the house.[12]

When the Fleet Street site was no longer capable of meeting the demand for electricity in the city, the Pigeon House plant emerged at Poolbeg in its place, replacing Fleet Street in 1903. The historic

---

11 Patrick Meehan, 'Early Dublin Public Lighting', *Dublin Historical Record* (Volume 5, Number 4), 130–6, at 135. 12 *ESB Prospect*, November 1981. With thanks to ESB Archives for digitisation of this and other materials.

Pigeon House plant is still there today, dwarfed by the red and white chimneys of the neighbouring contemporary site. 'Although no longer in use,' architectural historian Emma Gilleece notes, 'they stand as remnants of a key stage in the story of the powering, heating and lighting of Dublin city changing from coal to oil to gas.'[13] They have become a somewhat unlikely but iconic symbol of the city.

Electricity had arrived on our streets and in our homes. It transformed the lives of people in urban centres everywhere, with the horse-drawn tram giving way to something more efficient, and the streetscape brighter than before after dark. *The Irish Builder*, a leading voice in all things planning and development, insisted in 1881 that 'electricity will supersede gas in time, not only for lighting but also for heating, and who knows for how many other purposes? Possibly it may yet, even in our own time, supersede steam and the stream engine itself.'[14] It was certainly an understatement, in a century of extraordinary advancement for our cities.

Still, the replacement of gas lighting with electricity would be gradual, ensuring that in the popular imagination, the Victorian city remains defined by the gaslit streets. The writer F.J. Little, reflecting on growing up in the Victorian city, recounted Dublin as a place of:

Mystery at night, when feeble batswing gas-burners disclosed, without enlightening, cavernous lanes and obscure alleys where the shadow of the dreadful Past seemed to link arms with the dark forecast of a doubtful Future.

---

13 Emma Gilleece, '100 Buildings: How the Poolbeg Chimneys Became a Dublin Icon', https://www.rte.ie/culture/2021/1106/1256238-100-buildings-how-the-poolbeg-chimneys-became-a-dublin-icon/]]
14 *The Irish Builder*, 15 December 1881.

Shamrock detail visible in an electric lamp standard in Dublin city today (Luke Fallon).

CHAPTER TWO

From Deer to the People:
The Phoenix Park

On the 29th of May, 1453, the city of Constantinople fell to the troops of Mahomet II … In due course the smoke dispersed; Constantinople settled down to its long Ottoman repose; the scholars, hospitably received at western courts, left their manuscripts in the libraries of Rome and Milan. Like a seismic ripple or the last reverberation of a tidal wave, this great Levantine catastrophe spread its wings until, two hundred years later, a little wave washed up the stands of a remote western

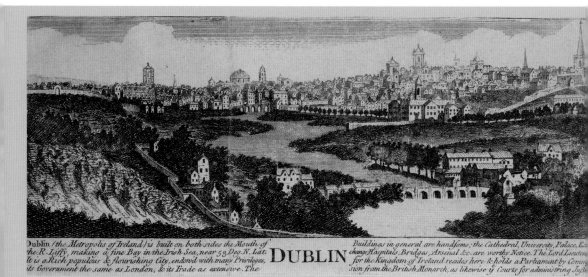

Text within the image:
Dublin (the Metropolis of Ireland) is built on both sides the Mouth of the R. Liffy, making a fine Bay in the Irish Sea, near 53 Deg. N. Lat. It is a Rich populous & flourishing City, endow'd with many Privileges, its Government the same as London, & its Trade as extensive. The

DUBLIN

Buildings in general are handsome; the Cathedral, University, Palace, &c change Hospitals, Bridges, Arsenal &c. are worthy Notice. The Lord Lieuten for the Kingdom of Ireland resides here & holds a Parliament by Comm sion from the British Monarch, as likewise of Courts for administring Justi

'Dublin and Islandbridge from the Magazine Hill in Phoenix Park', a view of the 'Metropolis of Ireland' from the Phoenix Park, c. eighteenth century (Courtesy of National Gallery of Ireland).

shore, and James Duke of Ormond stepped out of his pinnace onto the sands of Dublin Bay. The Renaissance, in a word, had arrived in Ireland. It was July the 27th in the year 1662.[1]

For Maurice Craig, Dublin's great architectural historian, the return of James Butler to Ireland in 1662 was nothing less than the arrival of the Renaissance to Irish shores.

Butler, the Duke of Ormond, had wisely sought safety in exile in the previous decade, along with King Charles II. A leading nobleman of the 'Old English' aristocracy in Ireland, he had commandeered a government army in Ireland before political changes in Britain forced him to seek refuge on the European continent.

Loyal to King Charles I, who had met his end in a public execution in January 1649, Ormond had unsuccessfully attempted

---

1 Maurice Craig, *Dublin 1660–1860* (Dublin, 1969), 3.

The Duke of Ormond by William Wissing (c. 1680–5) (Public Domain).

to prevent the conquest of Ireland by Oliver Cromwell. It was only with the Stuart Restoration of 1660, which brought King Charles II home from European exile, that Ormond could safely return to Ireland. Now, as viceroy, he set about a great reimagining of Dublin.

The influence of Paris was evident, and Frank McDonald writes of how it:

> ... promoted him to decree that henceforth buildings along the River Liffey would have to face the river on quays – as they did along the Seine – rather than turn their backs on it, as they had done until then. That is why, and deservedly so, the longest stretch of the Liffey quays perpetuate the ducal name in Ormond Quay Upper and Lower, as a tribute to his Paris-inspired vision.[2]

The Dublin that Ormond returned home to, at the beginning of the 1660s, was a city about one-sixth of the area of London. Its population, according to a census of 1659, stood at under nine thousand. Now came a time of tremendous change, and the making of a capital which would feel powerful. 'The first and greatest of these undertakings,' Craig notes, 'was the formation of the Phoenix Park.'[3] If Dublin was to be transformed from a mediaeval city to a metropolis, and something which could emulate the great European cities, the Phoenix Park was at the centre of such a project.

Centuries later, Ormond's interventions were still observed. The writer V.S. Pritchett observed how there were still 'aspects of foreign appearance in the city. The quays of the Liffey do recall (but in a decaying, mournful way) the quays of the Seine.'[4]

For the smaller metropolis of Dublin, London was always a city to emulate, and a blueprint of what a city could hope to become. Bragging rights, however, went to the smaller city with regard to parks. Regent's Park, Hyde Park, Kensington Gardens, St James's Park, Battersea Park and Greenwich Park are all beautiful and familiar landscapes. The Phoenix Park, at 1,752 acres, could comfortably

---

2 Frank McDonald, *A Little History of the Future of Dublin* (Dublin, 2021), 3. 3 Craig, *Dublin 1660–1860*, 13. 4 V.S. Pritchett, *Dublin: A Portrait* (London, 1967), 23.

Amidst a changing Phoenix Park, deer have been a constant. This sign on Chesterfield Avenue encourages drivers to be mindful of their presence (Luke Fallon).

absorb them all. It was a fact Vincent Caprani, a young 'journeyman letterpress machineman in the printing department of London's Savoy Hotel in 1959', enjoyed sharing with a Cockney workmate. 'He didn't, of course, believe me ... Why should he? London was the centre of his world. Dublin was mine.'[5] Caprani was correct.

This park in Dublin can only be understood when you are aware of the broader context of what was happening in Restoration Britain. John McCullen, in his history of the first two centuries of the Phoenix Park, notes that King Charles II and his court 'set about restoring royal and noble parks, having been influenced by their exile in France. Thus commenced the era of great formal landscapes which were characterised by extensive avenues and broad expanses of grass and water.'[6]

5 Vincent Caprani, *A Walk Around Dublin* (Dublin, 1992)   6 John McCullen, *An Illustrated History of the Phoenix Park: Landscape and Management to 1880* (Dublin, 2009), 16.

Phoenix Park deer today. The initial deer for the park were imported from England (Luke Fallon).

The Phoenix Park gradually grew. Still, some of what was originally considered within it, for example parts of Kilmainham, is no longer part of the park. The total cost of acquiring land ran to more than £40,000. The park was to be a royal deer park, an enclosed space not unlike Richmond Park and other such green spaces in England, which were stocked with fallow or red deer. Partridges, pheasants and deer from England were acquired for the park.

While it was reported in the early seventeenth century that Ireland yielded 'some reasonable plenty of fallow deer', which were said to be 'running loose in the woods of the north, of Leix and of Munster', it remained common to import deer from England.[7] The purpose of all of this was the creation of a hunting ground for royalty. The walls were as much to deter poachers as they were to keep animals within the space. Paul Rouse, in his landmark survey history of Irish sport, gives due space to hunting and describes how 'three keepers – one appointed a park ranger – were employed to protect further against poachers (though not always successfully). The park was then used for hunting as large and fashionable crowds followed the chase on horseback in the last decades of the seventeenth century.'[8] A space now thought of as fundamentally democratic, where sport belongs to any children with jumpers for goalposts, was founded as something else entirely.

The deer are a living link to the park of Ormond. Highly social animals, fallow deer move in large groups and have long attracted the attention of visitors. One such writer, in Victorian times, recounted:

> Close at hand lay two fine bucks, and I marvel at their apparent good-fellowship, knowing the habits of the animal in October. While mentally attributing their strange quietude

---

7 Terence Reeves Smith, 'A History of Deer Management in Ireland with Special Reference to the Glenarm Deer Parks', *Ulster Journal of Archaeology* (Volume 74, 2017), 231–58. 8 Paul Rouse, *Sport and Ireland: A History* (Oxford, 2015), 36–7.

Deer at leisure in the Phoenix Park, from the archives of Fáilte Ireland (Courtesy of Dublin City Library and Archive).

to the fact they are Irish, and of course different from any other bucks, they both rise together, and I then see that the two have been combatants, fighting until, like the warriors of old, they have lain down to rest, mutually exhausted.[9]

If the Phoenix Park can be understood as one of the defining changes to the Dublin of the seventeenth century, its development in the

---

9 George Rooper, *A Month in Mayo: With Miscellaneous Papers* (London, 1876), 120.

THE LAMPLIGHTERS OF THE PHOENIX PARK

The Viceregal Lodge, depicted with deer in foreground (Courtesy of National Library of Ireland).

following century also says much about the changing city, and its place within the British empire. Eighteenth-century interventions into the built environment of the park reflect the political and military realities of the day. Extensive use of the park by the military, and the arrival of a number of lodges and other buildings utilised by British officialdom in Ireland, lent a new feeling to the park.

Philip Dormer Stanhope, 4th Earl of Chesterfield by Allan Ramsay (Public Domain).

One building which embodies that change is the one we know today as Áras an Uachtaráin, but which once belonged to the park ranger. The house was partly designed by Nathaniel Clements, who was appointed to that post in 1751. Clements, in the words of his biographer, was an 'enlightened patron of architecture, not a practising architect', but he was still involved in bringing about and financing architectural change.[10] Clements has left an interesting architectural legacy in Dublin, having been involved too in the development of Henrietta Street, and the construction of at least five houses there. In 1782, the home constructed for Clements in the Phoenix Park was acquired by the government and became the Viceregal Lodge, a residence for the lord lieutenant of Ireland. Other lodges in the park would subsequently be acquired to house the chief secretary and the under-secretary. The Phoenix Park thus became, in the popular mind, part of a landscape that included Dublin Castle, the parliament on College Green and other sites synonymous with British rule.

While Ormond was the defining figure of the seventeenth-century Phoenix Park, the following century is deeply synonymous with the 4th Earl of Chesterfield, Philip Dormer Stanhope, who lends his name both to Chesterfield Avenue in the park, and to Stanhope Street in neighbouring Dublin 7. While Chesterfield's reign as lord lieutenant of Ireland was brief, spanning from 1745 into the following year, it was an interesting time for the Phoenix Park. Changes included the arrival of the Phoenix monument, a freestanding Portland stone Corinthian column, complete with stone phoenix and now a central feature of the park near Áras an Uachtaráin. There remains much mystery around the design of the Phoenix monument, but Chesterfield ensured his own immortality in the story of the park with an inscription that proclaims:

Civium oblectamento
Campum rudem et incultum

---

10 A.P.W. Malcomson, *Nathaniel Clements 1705–77: Politics, Fashion and Architecture in Mid-Eighteenth-Century Ireland* (Dublin, 2015).

Ornari jussit
Philippus Stanhope
Comes de Chesterfield
Prorex

Translated, it tells us: 'Philip Stanhope, Earl of Chesterfield, lord lieutenant, ordered this wild and uncultivated land to be ornamented for the pleasure of the citizens.'

The Phoenix in the Park, Dublin, J. Newman & Co., fl. 1838-1880 (Courtesy of National Library of Ireland).

The immortal phoenix, drawn from mythology, bears such little resemblance to the figure on top of the column that it instead became 'the eagle' in the minds of many. In a characteristic moment of light-hearted devilment, Senator Oliver St. John Gogarty attempted to have this bird included in the Wild Birds Protection Bill, brought before the house in 1929: 'There is one bird omitted from the Bill, and its omission is extraordinary ... I think something ought to be done to prevent people from shooting it.' Ironically, and as a later chapter will demonstrate, it proved to be one of the more secure monuments in the Phoenix Park.[11] In its own way, the monument has contributed to the debate surrounding the origin of the park's name, with general agreement from place-name authorities that the name owes more to the Irish language *fionn-uisce*, or clear water, than any mythological bird. In a poem commissioned at the time of European Union expansion in 2004, Nobel Prize laureate Seamus Heaney toyed with both meanings:

> *From middle sea to north sea, shining clear.*
> *As Phoenix flame upon fionn uisce here.*[12]

The park was certainly changing, and as McCullen notes, Chesterfield was central to the great journey to public accessibility. While London's Hyde Park had opened its gates in the 1630s, more than a century later 'only the carriages of persons of distinction were admitted to the Phoenix Park, in the fawning season, on orders signed by the Park bailiff'.[13] 1747 would see the formal opening of the Phoenix Park as a public space, but by the late eighteenth century, some were complaining of this new age of accessibility:

Under the rule of Mr Clements every impropriety was rigorously expelled from that beautiful spot. Ill-looking strollers of either

---

11 Seanad Éireann debate, 12 December 1929 (Houses of the Oireachtas. Volume 13, Number 7). 12 Chris Morash, *Dublin: A Writer's City* (Cambridge, 2023), 243. 13 McCullen, *An Illustrated History of the Phoenix Park,* 50.

THE PHENIX PILLAR, PHENIX PARK,
ERECTED 1745 BY PHILIP DORMER STANHOPE, EARL OF CHESTERFIELD.

Drawn by Geo. Petrie, Esq. R.H.A.

Engraved by B.Winkles.

Fisher, Son & Cº London, 1840

George Petrie's drawing of The Phoenix Pillar, Phoenix Park, Dublin, 1840 (Presented by Dr E. MacDowel Cosgrave, 1907, Courtesy of National Library of Ireland).

The Phoenix monument and gas lamp today. In the 1980s, the monument was moved back to the centre of Chesterfield Avenue (Luke Fallon).

Air Corps image showing the Phoenix Park Magazine Fort during the years of the Second World War (Military Archives).

sex could never get admittance at the gate except on public occasions ... But now, the gates are opened, wide to Tag, Rag and Bobtail. The Sabbath is abused by permitting a hurling match to be played there every Sunday evening, which is productive of blasphemous speaking, riot, drunkenness, broken heads and dislocated bones, among ten thousand of the lower class; and meanwhile the deer are hunted by detached parties of these vagrants and their dogs.[14]

We see the eighteenth century's imprint across the Phoenix Park, for example in the Magazine Fort, strategically positioned on a hill off the Military Road and offering great views across the city. Built on the orders of the lord lieutenant in the 1730s to designs by engineer John Corneille, its construction led to famous condemnation by none other than Dr Jonathan Swift:

> *Now's here's a proof of Irish sense*
> *Here Irish wit is seen*
> *When nothing's left that's worth defence*
> *We build a Magazine.*[15]

While Chesterfield Avenue may be named for the prior-mentioned earl, it owes its appearance now, like so much of the Phoenix Park, to Decimus Burton. The great nineteenth-century English architect and landscaper – and founding member of the Royal Institute of British Architects – brought to the park 'landscape restoration, the building of new gate lodges, tree planting, the construction of new roads and the realignment of others, as well as the restoration of the park's boundary wall'.[16] Burton's impact on London spaces includes the significant renovation of Hyde Park in the 1820s, London Zoo (where many of Burton's original buildings survive today) and the relocation of the Marble Archfrom Buckingham Palace to the north-east corner of Hyde Park, where it stands today. As an urban planner, Burton's impact on London was significant, and his many

---

14 Quoted in Thomas Pakenham and Valerie Pakenham (eds), *Dublin: A Traveller's Reader* (London, 2003) 106. **15** These words are sometimes disputed. They were attributed to Jonathan Swift when raised in parliament in 1820; see *Cobbett's Parliamentary Debates* (1820) **16** See *Parks: Our Shared Heritage* (Meath, 2017), produced to coincide with the exhibition of the same name which ran in Farmleigh and at The Mall Galleries, London in 2017.

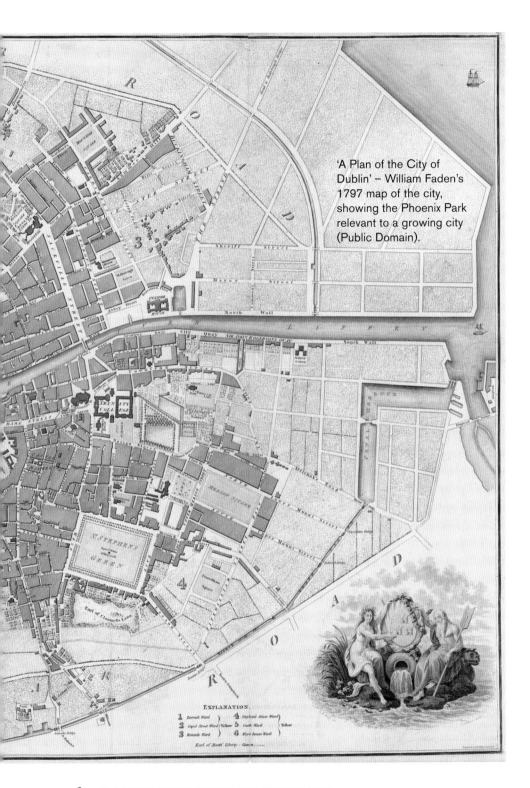

'A Plan of the City of Dublin' – William Faden's 1797 map of the city, showing the Phoenix Park relevant to a growing city (Public Domain).

Decimus Burton,
*Illustrated
London News*
(Alamy).

surviving interventions in the Phoenix Park are further testament
to his importance. His work in the London and Dublin parks, Dana
Arnold notes, 'made a substantial contribution to the re-imagining of
both cities and demonstrates how the principles of landscape design
used in rural environments were easily imported into a metropolitan
context'.[17]

17 Dana Arnold, *Rural Urbanism: London Landscapes in the Early Nineteenth Century* (Manchester, 2005), 69.

The Burton era and its immediate aftermath witnessed the arrival of the Zoological Gardens, the People's Garden (a classic Victorian flower garden), the bandstand in the Hollow and other additions which added to the park as a space of recreation and enjoyment for the people of Dublin and beyond. It was into this environment that the Flanagan family arrived as lamplighters in 1890.

A sign for Gairdíní na Hainmhithe, the Zoological Gardens (Luke Fallon).

Nicholas Flanagan (Flanagan Family).

CHAPTER THREE

A Family Tradition

This was the last stronghold of gas here in Phoenix Park. I done me work and there was never one complaint against me in the fifty-one years I was in it ... You met every sort in the park ... old-age pensioners, the high-ups, the trams. On every road you went you met characters. It was a pleasure and I was me own boss. And if it was a good summer's morning and you're going down the main road there'd be a couple of buses laden with tourists coming along and the driver'd pull up and the next thing out come the cameras.

Tom Flanagan in conversation with Kevin C. Kearns

Dublin owes a debt of gratitude beyond words to Kevin C. Kearns, oral historian and cultural geographer.

Kearns, Professor at the University of Northern Colorado, spent decades capturing the voices of the Dublin working class, from market dealers to dockers, allowing the people of the city to tell their own stories. The tools of the trade, as he recently recalled it, were 'a sturdy Colorado mountain backpack stuffed with two small Sony tape recorders, extra batteries and cassettes, Pentax 35mm cameras and film, writing notebook, pens, detailed Dublin city street map, collapsible umbrella – and a package of McVitie's biscuits'. Keen not to be mistaken for another 'lost Yank tourist wandering the cityscape', he embarked on the most ambitious and far-reaching oral history of the city ever undertaken.[1] Over more than fifty years from 1969, Kearns interviewed hundreds of people. Some were reluctant to tell their stories; others opened up freely before the tape recorder. They told him of the years of the Emergency, the so-called Monto area of the city, famed policeman 'Lugs' Branigan, the infamous street-fighting 'Animal Gangs' and everything else imaginable from the lore of the city. His *Dublin Street Life and Lore*, published in 1991, begins with a quote from the landmark *Oral History: From Tape to Tape*, considered an essential guidebook of sorts to oral historians everywhere:

> Oral historians are haunted by the obituary page. Every death represents the loss of a potential narrator and thus an absolute diminution of society's collective historical memory.[2]

For Kearns, it was a race against time to tell the story of a city and its people. One of the voices he captured was that of Tom Flanagan, father of Frank and James, and a second-generation Phoenix Park

---

1 A recent collection of interviews captures the scale of work undertaken by Kearns. Kevin C. Kearns, *In Our Day: An Oral History of Dublin's Bygone Days* (Dublin, 2022) 2 Kevin C. Kearns, *Dublin Street Life and Lore* (Dublin, 1991), 6.

A view of the Phoenix Park as it would have appeared in the time of Nicholas Flanagan (Courtesy of National Library of Ireland).

lamplighter. In his eighties at the time Kearns interviewed him, Tom painted a picture of his own profession, and the fifty-one years he had spent at it: 'I worked till 1975. *Never bored once.*'[3] Tom followed in the footsteps of Nicholas Flanagan, his own father. Frank explains:

> In 1890 our grandfather, Nicholas Flanagan, and four of his brothers took on the job of servicing the lamps in the park. There was over three hundred lamps in it at the time, as there

---

3 Ibid., 77.

were gas lamps in all of the estates, as well as the roads of the park.

Today, the work of the Flanagans is largely restricted to Chesterfield Avenue and the roads immediately around it. In the Victorian age, however, before electricity had made its presence felt in the park, Nicholas and his brothers were in and out of the estates and offices of the park. They knew them as 'The Vice' (the Viceregal Lodge, later Áras an Uachtaráin), 'The Chiefs' (the chief secretary to the lord lieutenant of Ireland, later the home of the US ambassador) and 'The Unders' (the under-secretary to the lord lieutenant of Ireland, later the home of the papal nuncio).

It seems most likely that the door into a family profession was opened by Patrick Baggot, an influential figure in the local area, commemorated today with the naming of Baggot Road, near the Flanagan home. Baggot, a developer and politician, would serve for many years on the North Dublin Rural Council. Walking to

A cyclist posing at the Phoenix Column (Courtesy of National Library of Ireland).

Nicholas Flanagan
and family
(Flanagan Family).

the Flanagan family home for the first time down Baggot Road, I wondered if it had any connection to Baggot Street in the city centre, named for Robert Bagod of the thirteenth century, but this story is instead very local. According to Frank, 'Baggot owned all the land around here. He owned the twenty cottages up there, and Nicholas got his pick of them.'

Baggot was a popular local figure, more interested in the affairs of the locality than the bigger picture of national politics. In some ways, he sounds akin to an Alfie Byrne of Blackhorse Avenue. Byrne,

Baggot Terrace on Blackhorse Avenue remains a testament to the contribution of the family to the area (Luke Fallon).

a popular politician in the city centre, would serve as lord mayor on ten occasions. A constant presence in the 1930s, he was so good at engaging with people on the ground, he earned the moniker 'the Shaking Hand of Dublin'.[4] In the newspaper archives we find reference to Baggot over a number of decades, fighting local battles such as the case of a dismissed street sweeper:

> Mr Baggot said a man named Redmond, who had been employed in Blackhorse Road for the past year and had given good service as a sweeper, had been notified of his dismissal. This man was a resident of the district and his place was being filled by a man from Blanchardstown ... the dismissal of Redmond meant that no man resident in the district was

---

4 Trevor White, *Alfie: The Life and Times of Alfie Byrne* (Dublin, 2017).

given employment by the County in the district of Blackhorse Road or in any other district and a large number of the occupants of the hundred labourers' cottages in the district were unemployed. Redmond was the sole support of two invalid sisters ... Mr Baggot said the system which led to the dismissal of a good man like Redmond and left local men unemployed whilst men were imported from other districts was wrong.[5]

Redmond got his job back, and Baggot – we can only presume – gained or solidified a vote. Through the provision of labourers' cottages in the locality, Baggot's name emerges repeatedly in late nineteenth- and early twentieth-century coverage of housing issues in that part of the city. The period witnessed very real philanthropic and semi-philanthropic efforts to address the housing crisis, including the Dublin Artisans' Dwellings Company and the Guinness-founded Iveagh Trust.[6] Much analysis of the crisis then impacting Dublin focused on the high density of tenement areas, and put hope in suburbanisation and moving people to newly constructed houses and cottages in places like Cabra, near to the Phoenix Park. It's clear that the North Dublin Rural Council faced its own housing issues. A letter from a local man, read out at a meeting attended by Baggot and other councillors, highlighted the gravity of the situation: 'I am living in an outhouse with my wife and three children. I could not pay the rent of the hut I was in.'[7] Families like the Flanagans benefited from Baggot's efforts locally.

Before his career as a lamplighter, Nicholas Flanagan had worked as a labourer in a variety of settings. Frank remembers him as a sort of jack-of-all-trades as well as working the Phoenix Park job. He was good with animals, and had worked on a number of local estates. 'Another

---

5 *Drogheda Independent*, 24 November 1928. **6** Murray Fraser, *John Bull's Other Homes: State Housing and British Policy in Ireland 1883–1922* (Liverpool, 1996). **7** *Drogheda Independent*, 21 December 1929.

thing he used to do is pull teeth, before anaesthetic or anything like it. If someone knocked on the door with a bottle of whiskey in his hand they'd go out to the shed. You'd hear the roars from the shed, and both of them, naturally, would have a swig of the whiskey.'

The Phoenix Park that Nicholas and his brothers began working in during the late Victorian period was an exciting place, bustling with people, and not all of them in search of recreation. The park was increasingly utilised as a space for political demonstrations in the 1890s. At a time when the Irish Parliamentary Party was in crisis, owing to the scandal and fallout surrounding Charles Stewart Parnell's relationship with Katharine O'Shea, the estranged wife of a fellow IPP parliamentarian with whom Parnell had fallen in love, the gatherings could sometimes turn heated. During one demonstration, at which 'several bands were present, and the Lord Mayor moved the first resolution, which affirmed that Mr Parnell was alone fitted to lead the Irish nation', an effigy of Parnell's political opponent Tim Healy was burnt, 'the crowd afterwards kicking the remnants about the ground'.[8] There were sizeable May Day rallies, a day traditionally associated with the labour movement. Some of these were addressed by figures as diverse as Eleanor Marx (daughter of the political philosopher Karl Marx) and Michael Canty, the Dublin organiser of the National Union of Gasworkers and General Labourers.

The park was also increasingly becoming a place of recreation for ordinary Dubliners, with the rise of association football and other sports in the city. In the very year that the Flanagans began their job, Bohemian Football Club (Bohs) was born in a gate lodge house of the park, beside the North Circular Road. Strongly connected to the Royal Hibernian Military School, located within the Phoenix Park, Bohs represented the coming together of two things that were synonymous with the place: sport and the garrison. The Phoenix Park

---

8 *Belfast News Letter*, 8 December 1890.

The Hole in the Wall public house. Still in operation today, former names have included the Blackhorse Tavern and Nancy Hands (Courtesy of National Library of Ireland).

became a magnet for the game of soccer in Dublin, historian Paul Rouse detailing how, owing to this rising popularity:

> In 1901 the Commissioners of the Public Works laid out soccer pitches in the Phoenix Park ... Within a year, they had received 1,000 applications for their use, growing to 3,000 by 1904. Such was the demand for soccer in Dublin that by 1906 the Phoenix Park was home to twenty-nine soccer pitches; by contrast, there were just two for Gaelic games.[9]

Michael Cusack, founder of the Gaelic Athletic Association, would denounce 'the foreign faction, the Orange Catholics [and] the West

---

9 Rouse, *Sport and Ireland: A History*, 214.

A later image of families from the area, many with strong working connections to the Phoenix Park, drinking in the same premises (Flanagan Family).

Britons who played association football in Dublin's Phoenix Park'.[10] Political demonstrators, temperance advocates, members of the city's marching bands, soccer aficionados and lamplighters were all in the milieu of those crossing the park on any day, alongside the bureaucracy of the British state, military and policing in Ireland. The presence of soldiers in and around the park impacted life in the area in sometimes surprising ways – and has entered local folklore. Take the Hole in the Wall pub on Blackhorse Avenue, an unusual name that perhaps suggests a quaint little pub, leading to surprise on seeing the scale

10 Neal Garnham, *Association Football and Society in Pre-partition Ireland* (Belfast, 2004), 135.

of the establishment, one of the longest public house premises of its kind. It is instead said to be named in honour of a tradition whereby drink was served through a hole in the wall to members of the army garrison stationed in the park, a contested theory in its own right, but an enduring one.

Nicholas and his brothers went out no matter what the elements threw at them. As Frank remembers:

> They worked seven days a week, in all weather. No matter what the weather was, they had to go out in it. They generally wore a cornsack, a way of protecting themselves from the elements ... they all remembered the big storm in 1903, when hundreds upon hundreds of trees were taken out of it. I can recall Nicholas saying as many as three thousand trees were lost to the storm.

There is no exaggeration in how Frank recounts the night. A newspaper report tells us:

> Last night's storm in Dublin was the most severe in living memory, and the damage was immense and widespread ... An unoccupied house at 57 Mabbot Street fell, two derelict houses collapsed in Spitalfields, and a house was blown down at 1 New Row South ... Among the localities that suffered most was the Phoenix Park. Here trees were torn up and levelled by the hundreds. In one section of the Park alone over five hundred trees were laid prone, and all the roads were strewn with boughs and branches.[11]

The brothers returned to work the next day, to find many of the lamps badly damaged and in need of repair. James Joyce references the

---

11 *Irish Examiner*, 28 February 1903.

storm in *Ulysses*, in which a character wanders through the Phoenix Park reflecting on it: 'Lady Dudley was walking home through the park to see all the trees that were blown down by that cyclone last year and thought she'd buy a view of Dublin.[12]'

The manner in which Nicholas and his brothers worked was different from that of the Flanagans today, as the technology had not yet advanced as far as time switches. James, always interested in the development of the gas lamps, speaks of how:

> They were each supplied with a pole, and there was a trap door in the bottom of the lamp. There was a carbide tip on the top of the pole with a hook, which they'd push through the bottom of the lamps. There were no timers on them yet. So in the morning they'd go out and do the same again.

In that sense, it was a much more laborious job, before the introduction of timers which would bring the lights on automatically at the same time each evening. The timers themselves brought the need to learn new skills, but removed one daily routine.

The Flanagan brothers worked in the Phoenix Park throughout the revolutionary period, when the park and its immediate surroundings were the scene of some dramatic events. The park saw major demonstrations during the 1913 Lockout, a labour dispute which pitted the trade union organiser James Larkin against William Martin Murphy, amongst the city's largest employers and deeply hostile to Larkin's style of union organisation. Frank recounted how: 'My father was a great follower of Larkin's, as were all the gasmen. They regarded him as a saviour, and of course he was a great speaker. My father would always go to Jim's meetings.' Jim Larkin's newspaper, *The Irish Worker*, frequently gave space to lamplighters in the city and their grievances.

---

12 Daniel Mulhall, *Ulysses, A Reader's Odyssey*, New Island Books, 2022.

When rebellion came at Easter 1916, the intended signal that the insurrection had begun was to be the blowing up of the Magazine Fort in the park. A member of the republican boy scouts, Na Fianna Éireann, later remembered of his comrades:

> They proceeded to the Phoenix Park on bicycles and two hackney cars, disguised as footballers. Idly kicking the ball up the slopes, surrounding the Fort, two or three of the 'players' came close to the British sentry at the gate, held him up with revolvers, the main body rushed in, disarmed the guard, cut the telephone, and the Fort was captured. Small parties of the raiding force at once entered the ammunition stores, and set them on fire. They then withdrew in accordance with their order, and reported to the Four Courts.[13]

The Rising brought a strange feeling to the park. The Flanagans continued to light the gas lamps, but access to the park was greatly restricted. It remained a dangerous place to be throughout the week, and there is still much mystery around the death of Richard Butler, shot in the People's Gardens on the third day of the insurrection.[14]

In Dublin Zoo, there was a deep sense of crisis. With the superintendent of the zoo, Dr Benjamin Banks Ferrar, drafted in to treat the injured in a city-centre hospital, the job of maintaining the institution fell on the shoulders of his wife Isabella and three young zookeepers who stayed to help her. In time, the remains of a number of horses killed in the fighting were brought to the zoo.

The Flanagans had a lucky escape in December 1919, the period of the War of Independence, when an IRA ambushing party opened fire on Lord French, the lord lieutenant of Ireland, who they regarded

---

13 Taken from Witness Statement WS1377, by Aodh MacNeill, part of the Bureau of Military History collection, courtesy of the Military Archives, Ireland. 14 Eunan O'Halpin and Daithí Ó Corráin, *The Dead of the Irish Revolution* (Dublin, 2020), 52.

'The car in which Lord French was ambushed' – W.D. Hogan image of the aftermath of the raid, with a soldier pointing out a bullet hole (Courtesy of National Library of Ireland).

as a ruthless military opponent. At Ashtown Cross, just outside the walls of the Phoenix Park, a waiting party that included the famed IRA leader Dan Breen opened fire on a convoy of vehicles, though mistaken intelligence information had meant they fired on the wrong car. 'Drive like the devil!' shouted Sergeant Hally, a detective who was with Lord French. The driver did. Tom Flanagan, Frank remembers, 'had to make way for a speeding car on the Odd Lamp Road'. A memorial to IRA volunteer Martin Savage, killed in the shootout, marks the spot at Ashtown today.

French brushed off the concern of the prime minister and others for his well-being: 'They are bad shots.'[15] Vincent Byrne, one of the

---

15 *The Irish Times*, 21 January 2019.

ambushing party, later recalled his own surprise at getting away from the scene:

> We proceeded along the Navan Road. As I was cycling by myself, I started talking to myself, in the strain that we would never see town. I honestly believed that we would never make the city, because I thought that the word of the attack would have been received by the military station in Marlboro' Barracks (now known as McKee Barracks), and that they would cut us off at a turning at the right-hand side. However, Dame Luck was with us.[16]

Young Tom Flanagan had avoided the speeding car, but three years later he encountered evidence of another fight. The remnants of artillery shell were found on the Odd Lamp Road – it had gone astray of its target during the Free State forces' bombardment of the occupied Four Courts in the dramatic opening salvos of the Civil War. It was a souvenir not to be envied: 'George Pennycot, a colleague, took it home,' Frank recalls.

There were other risks in the Phoenix Park too. 'On more than one occasion,' Frank recalled of the earlier lamplighters, 'they were challenged at gunpoint.' During the Irish War of Independence, which raged from 1919 until 1921, the Royal Irish Constabulary depot in the park was home to the much feared 'Auxies', or Auxiliary Cadets, recruited against the backdrop of the developing conflict. Built as a training depot in 1842 by architect Jacob Owens, the building today serves as the headquarters of An Garda Síochána. With a number of attacks on military and police taking place in the vicinity of the Phoenix Park, there was little trust in anyone encountered within it.

In the city centre, lamplighters working a very different beat from

---

16 Taken from Witness Statement WS423, by Vincent Byrne, part of the Bureau of Military History collection, courtesy of the Military Archives, Ireland.

(left) A memorial to Martin Savage at Ashtown today (Luke Fallon); (opposite) 'On Ashtown Road', a song written in honour of Martin Savage and published immediately after the events (Courtesy National Library of Ireland).

the Flanagans could find themselves entangled in the events of the revolution. In a city that was frequently in curfew, they were amongst the few workers who had the freedom of the streets at night. One, Frank Wearen, recalled:

> Lamplighters knew everything. Everything. They seen everything. But they kept their mouth shut. And there were a few of them in the Movement, too, you know ... Oh, they

On Ashtown Road,

Martin Savage, I.R.A., Killed in Action December 19th, 1919.

Air: "Snowy Breasted Pearl."

One cold December Day,
A motor ploughed its way,
Mid bullets flash and play,
 On Ashtown Road.

In that car a living tool,
Of England's hated rule,
And there began a duel
 On Ashtown Road.

Young Savage undismayed,
With bomb and hand grenade,
Attacked them unafraid
 On Ashtown Road.

But a bullet laid him low,
From the rifles of the foe,
Ye another debt we owe
 For Ashtown Road.

Who dies for Ireland lives,
For her their life blood gives,
As this noble lad gave his
 On Ashtown Road·

They laid him in the grave,
Where leafless branches wave,
Oh! son of Erin brave,
 Farewell to thee.

were very useful. If it was curfew they'd be stopped by the Black and Tans. But you carried a permit when you're a night worker in the Corporation and they'd let you go. They always carried a bunch of keys for opening the lamps and they could open a lamp and shove a gun into it and shut it if they were after doing a job. That took place.[17]

While Chesterfield Avenue was a relatively quiet place when the Flanagan family were doing their rounds, the city lamplighters worked in a more bustling environment. Wearen joked of how 'you'd carry your pole over your shoulder like a rifle, like a soldier. You'd hold it standing up, not sticking out, so no one would run into it.'[18]

Post-independence, things changed rapidly in the Phoenix Park. There was symbolic change, as the old order gave way to the new Free State. From the Royal Hibernian Military School in the park, soldiers from British regiments bid farewell:

> The Northamptons and the Royal Welsh Fusiliers, in full kit, with fixed bayonets and with subalterns carrying the regimental colours, paraded yesterday in the great square in the front buildings and, while the Free State guard presented arms, marched away out of the gate through Phoenix Park, their bands playing farewell.[19]

One tongue-in-cheek guidebook to 1920s Dublin drew attention to who was now living in what were once the homes of the British political and military elite in Ireland:

> When visiting the Phoenix Park, sir, you must halt your touring car to gaze for a moment at a grey, flat-faced building,

---

17 Kearns, *Dublin Street Life and Lore*, 75. **18** Ibid. **19** *Belfast News Letter*, 16 December 1922.

which has memories beginning with the elegant Philip Stanhope, Earl of Chesterfield, and ending with the martial John French, Earl of Ypres. Once upon a time a lean, fiery-eyed, acid-tongued young man called Tim Healy referred to it as a 'den of iniquity'. Today it is occupied by a rather solemn, portly, but still acid-tongued old gentleman named the Right Honourable Timothy Michael Healy.[20]

Things were changing for the lamplighters too. While the park had resisted the arrival of electric lighting in the way the city had embraced it, technological developments meant that gas lamps themselves were changing. As James tells it, 'The arrival of the timers was a real game-changer, not only in the Phoenix Park but across the city of Dublin. It left a lot of men out of work.' The timers constituted a clockwork mechanism which rotated at its set time to lift a lever, turning the gas on and off. The initial timers were seven days, eventually giving way to the fourteen-day timers still in use today.

The Flanagan firm was reduced significantly, down to just Nicholas and his son Tom, who remembered his pride at keeping on the tradition:

> Now, I was taken on as a helper for me father. I was seventeen. Oh, there's no doubt about it, I was the proudest man in the world when I started. I got one pound fifteen a week and I was doing immense! And I got a bicycle, a blaze-red bicycle. I was on the bicycle fifty-one years. Oh, not the same bicycle. I had three or four bicycles. They were ordinary standard Raleigh bikes. And I went through a good many tyres as well, I'd say. I had no uniform but I always wore a coat and tie. I always felt you were never dressed without a tie.[21]

---

20 M.J. McManus, *So This Is Dublin!* (Dublin, 1927), 16. 21 Kearns, *Dublin Street Life and Lore*, 76.

A young Tom Flanagan (Flanagan Family).

For Tom, there was a sense that he was amongst the very last workers of a tradition, recalling how 'it was the back streets and back lanes in Dublin that was the last lit with gas lamps'. There were increasing calls from business, local politicians and the press to move the city away from gas lights and towards electricity. One letter-writer to the *Evening Herald* in 1924, capturing the feeling of the time, complained of the state of lighting on her road in Drumcondra:

> The scattered gas lamps thereon at any time but served to intensify the darkness, but latterly, owing to defective or broken mantles, sections of the throughfare are plunged in Stygian gloom that would afford admirable lurking place for hold-ups. Considering the rateable value of the locality, is it not time that electric lights were installed?[22]

By then, the lamplighter was being written about as a fading curiosity of the streetscape. Readers of one newspaper in 1926 were told to look out for him, as he 'still potters along some lanes and alleys and byways of Dublin, although the principal streets have long been lighted by lofty globes, which mysteriously spring into life, all together, at the dusk and do not need his assistance'. That same piece captured something about the lights, describing how 'the most striking difference between gas light and electric light is that gas light preserves the human touch. A gas lamp standing in a street, even with the gas turned on, is a dead, futile, cold thing until the lamplighter comes along to touch it into genial, friendly light.' That sense of the transformative power of the lamplighter is also found in the poetry of Máirtín Ó Direáin. The Aran Island poet, living in Dublin as a civil servant with little *grá* for the capital, found something magical in the process, referring to the lamplighter as a *draíodóir* (magician):

---

22 *Evening Herald*, 28 November 1924.

Ní raibh sé mór, an fear
Níor dheas a bhí ach gránna,
Is cóip an bhaile mhóir
Ag fonóid faoi gan náire,
Ach ghluais gan mhairg fós
Is ar chuaillí chuaigh in airde
Ba dhraíodóir an fear beag
A raibh an solas ina ghlaic,
É ag tabhairt na gile leis
Ó lampa go lampa sráide.[23]

For Dublin children, the lamps offered more than light, whether gas or electric. In his entertaining memoir of growing up in the city, John Mullee recounted how 'lampposts had other important uses for boys. For example, the base made a nice wicket for cricket games.'[24] On Mount Street Crescent in the heart of Dublin 2, Derek A. Fitzsimons has produced a bronze statue, 'Memories of Mount Street', which shows a child swinging out of a lamp standard from a rope. Technological advancements meant little in the democracy of street games. As long as the lamp standard itself remained, Dublin children would swing out of it.

If the newspapers of the 1920s had plenty of such sentimentality around the gas lamps, the defining feature of coverage of gas lamps in the subsequent decade was the retirement of lamplighters. There was Tommie Nolan, described in *The Irish Press* as 'Dublin's oldest lamplighter' in September 1937. Tommie, readers were told, was 'one of the fast-vanishing band which will soon have made way for Progress':

> In the twenty-three years he has flitted bat-like through the city's dismal streets and frowsy alleys, torch in hand, he has

---

23 Quoted in Charles J. Sullivan, *The Gasmakers: Historical Perspectives on the Irish Gas Industry* (Dublin, 1987), 1. 24 John Mullee, *Growing Up in Dublin: Reflections on the 1950s* (Dublin, 2015).

The Lamplighter public house in the Coombe, one of the last reminders of these workers in the city centre (Luke Flanagan).

lit a million lamps and put them all out again. All the night workers returning home on Tommie's beat know his friendly 'good morning', and all are grateful for it.

'Soon we'll have gone the way of the muffin man,' Tommie said. 'They are installing electric lamps all over the place. Still, it was an interesting job. All the extraordinary people you meet at night!'[25]

---

25 *The Irish Press*, 24 September 1937.

Tommie, at least, got to bow out in the pages of a national newspaper. There is something almost tragic about the report of the transition from gas to electricity in Balbriggan, where thirty years of service ended literally overnight:

> At their meeting, the Town Commissioners on Tuesday night decided to light the town by electricity, and on Wednesday morning I noticed the lamplighter dismantling the gas lamps. He has been 30 years in the service of the Commissioners as lamplighter and the dismantling of the lamps is probably his last job in this connection.[26]

These scenarios were playing out in towns and cities across Ireland and Britain, but not within the walls of the Phoenix Park. While lamplighters across the island were losing jobs, the Flanagans were busy working on some of the first major events hosted in the newly independent State. There was none bigger than the Eucharistic Congress, which was held in Dublin in June 1932. Hundreds of thousands assembled in the park for mass, at which Count John McCormack performed and a greeting from Pope Pius XI was broadcasted live from the Vatican to the gathered crowd. The Congress, in the words of one historian, 'provided a showcase for the strength of Irish faith, and the Irish people did not disappoint'[27]. For the Flanagan family, it was a showcase occasion too, bringing world leaders of the faith to Dublin. Frank remembers how 'Nicholas, the grandfather, was out of the business by then. But he went back into it for that. There was a big job to get it all looking right.' Though only a baby at the time, Frank remembers the stories that were passed on: 'They said it was such a fine week, most of the people didn't bother going home at all. Some just slept under

---

26 *Drogheda Independent*, 19 April 1930. 27 David G. Holmes, 'The Eucharistic Congress of 1932 and Irish Identity', *New Hibernia Review / Iris Éireannach Nua* Vol. 4, No. 1 (Spring, 2000), pp. 55–78, 55.

An image of High Mass in the Phoenix Park during the 1932 Eucharistic Congress (Courtesy of National Library of Ireland).

the trees during it. I remember too that our father, like many people around here, ended up with a tiny piece of the altar.'

If the Eucharistic Congress was something the new Free State could revel in, and a positive promotion for the city on the world stage, the end of the 1930s brought a moment of great embarrassment, moving the park once more to centre stage. The IRA's raid on the Magazine Fort, on 23 December 1939, led to its capture and the seizure of the munitions dump. Frank remembers his father and other men who worked in the park being taken aback by the boldness of the act. 'It was the night before Christmas Eve, which meant everyone was probably a little lax. I can remember my father and Con Delaney next door, both blown away by it.' Reading the recollections of one of the raiding party, Liam Ó Brádaigh, however, it may have been a little easier than Tom Flanagan and others might have imagined:

> We went on a tour of the fort, to acquaint ourselves with its layout, only as a matter of historical interest. During this period of our tenure, it was discovered that an army sentry was still patrolling one of the cat-walks on a rampart – evidently unaware that the fort was taken over! When approached by one of our men to hand up his rifle, he replied, still obviously unaware *who* was taking his rifle, that he still had a ½ hour stint to do before he was off sentry duty! We later found out he was only a raw recruit![28]

'People talked about commotion in the park that night,' Frank recalls. This fits with Ó Brádaigh's recollections, of a military lorry appearing on the scene at the very end of the raid: 'They were obviously confused as to what was going on – but before they could leave the lorry, I was able to discharge several shots over their heads, in order to warn the remaining occupants of the fort.'[29] While an embarrassment to the government of the day, much of the Magazine Fort munitions were quickly recovered.

Tom's life, in many ways, was like that of Nicholas before him. He still called Blackhorse Lane home, living with Esther Lane, who he married in 1931. By 1941, Frank recalls, 'they had six children'. Both were people of strong religious faith, and 'they both became daily communicants'. Within the Phoenix Park, some things were just as they had been in earlier times.

Just as his father and uncles had worked through the extreme

---

28 *A Libertarian of the Thirties* is the title of Liam Ó Brádaigh's fantastic memoir, which covers his working-class upbringing in the Liberties and his time in the IRA before his internment in the Curragh. It deserves a broader readership, and I'm grateful for having received a copy of the limited run. **29** Ibid.

weather of 1903, Tom worked throughout the 'big snow' of 1947, which brought extreme weather conditions to the entire country in February and March. 'Worst Blizzard for 25 Years Hits Ireland' was the *Irish Times* headline on the morning of 26 February. There was no let-up for several weeks, and as Dean Ruxton notes in a piece looking back at that time:

> Co. Wicklow bore the brunt of it. Residents of Rathdrum moved to call on the Irish Red Cross to fly food to them, because many had not been able to leave their homes for a month. By the end of the first week of March, a plan was hatched to have an RAF jet drop food parcels to villages in Wicklow, such was the extent of the road blockage.[30]

Tom remembered conditions in the park being unlike anything he'd encountered before. 'Icicles would be hanging off the lamps and you'd have to knock them off to open the lamp.' Tom had his own theories when it came to the weather, but as Frank recalls, so did other workers in the Phoenix Park. It seemed in each house around the park there was a unique theory explaining the weather:

> Billy Kinsella, the Ashtown gatekeeper, made his judgement based on trees, plants and birds for the weather. Bill 'Crow' Goddin, the last of 100 years of deer keepers in the park, read the movement of birds; the early swallows, the plover before hard weather, flights of jackdaws before a storm. Tom Newsom, who rode a bike with a carbide lamp, placed all his bets on the quarters of the moon. Tilted on its back meant bad weather, standing nearly vertical – good weather.

---

30 *The Irish Times*, 2 March 2018.

A 1969 snowy scene in the Phoenix Park, from the collections of Fáilte Ireland (Courtesy of Dublin City Library and Archive).

THE LAMPLIGHTERS OF THE PHOENIX PARK

During 1947's dismal weather, the Phoenix Park maintained its wartime appearance. The *Irish Independent* described the stockpiling that occurred there, for fear of shortages:

> Dubliners should stay warm this winter; the 70,000-ton coal dump at the Phoenix Park grows daily by four thousand tons, while turf clamps line the roads and sprawl like miniature mountain ranges across the grassland ... Pretty hard now to recognise the peaceful Sunday afternoon walks of a few years back.[31]

The Phoenix Park described is unrecognisable to us today. The report went on to describe the park as 'a teeming, throbbing hive of industry, when the bell-men appear this month to take delivery of their allocations the Phoenix Park will bear a strong resemblance to a Canadian lumber camp'.[32]

An old friend of Dublin's lamplighters, Jim Larkin, died during the period of extreme weather. The Irish labour movement had changed dramatically in the decades since Larkin's heyday, and his influence on the trade union leadership had been greatly reduced due to the emergence of more moderate leaders. Still, Larkin's past heroics had ensured his place in the folk memory of the city, and his was a funeral fit for a hero. The roads were covered in snow, and the city in a sort of paralysis, but Dublin felt it had to pay its respects. *The Irish Press* captured the feeling:

> There were crowds at Jim Larkin's funeral – just as there were crowds in Jim Larkin's life. A half century of history marched through Dublin yesterday morning ... They had all come out, men in dungarees with overcoats buttoned up to the throats.

---

31 *The Irish Press*, 13 October 1947.   32 Ibid.

It could have been a Citizen Army or Irish Volunteers parade, only for the slowness. The air of the city seemed to be muffled. And the men in the dungarees, and women grown old who have borne children since they struck instinctively at the 400 bosses at Larkin's will, seemed to be there because they just had to be there.[33]

It was a disciple of Larkin's, the novelist James Plunkett, who would place Dublin's lamplighters centrally into *Strumpet City* – his novel of life in Dublin at the time of the 1913 Lockout. *Strumpet City* is written with such intensity and attention to detail that one would be forgiven for presuming its author had come through the events himself – instead, Plunkett was born in 1920. A heroic saga that pits the workers of the city against its elites, Plunkett had a fantastic ability to evoke the sights and sounds of the city in his work. In the book's opening page he describes a royal visit to Dublin, and streets lit by 'Japanese lanterns and fairy-lights, thousands of coloured gas lamps'. Yet it is the descriptions of the ordinary days of the city that are the most impressive: 'A lamplighter just ahead of them went methodically about his work, reaching upwards with his long, light cane and leaving a glowing chain of lamps in his wake.'[34]

Tom himself emerges in some interesting places, captured not only in the important work of Kevin C. Kearns, but immortalised in song too. In the 2003 musical *A Man of No Importance*, a title with a nod towards Oscar Wilde, we encounter the song 'The Streets of Dublin', with mention for 'Tommy Flanagan who lights the gas lamps', and a chorus which honours him and other Dublin workers. The chorus speaks of the evocative nature of the gas lamps, how they draw feelings out of anyone who passes by them

---

33 *The Irish Press*, 5 February 1947.   34 James Plunkett's *Strumpet City* was chosen as Dublin's One City One Book choice for 2013, giving an indication of its importance in the literature of the city. First published by Hutchinson & Co., London, 1969.

and sees their light. At night, the lamps appear like something of a divine nature. Their glow is described as a welcome presence on Chesterfield Avenue.[35]

To Tom, the lights were something worth celebrating. Similarly to the song which championed him, he spoke of the warmth from the glow of the gas lights. To him, seeing light from gas lamps created the effect of light through a fog. 'With a gas light it's a warm glow. It sends the rays down like in a fog. Oh, a warm little glow. In the summer it was *excellent*.'[36] When the Phoenix Park gas lamps were restored and renovated in 1988, a journalist watching the spectacle felt compelled to note that 'the glow from the newly restored gas lamps in the Phoenix Park paled yesterday in comparison with the glow on the face of 81-year-old Tom Flanagan, who had lovingly tended the original lamps for more than half a century'.[37]

Beyond the lamplights, I asked Frank and James if there were other interesting branches on the family tree. What I didn't expect was a moment tied to the great excitement of Beatlemania sweeping Dublin in November 1963, when the Scouse sweethearts performed two gigs at the Adelphi Cinema on the same day. 'We'd two uncles that worked in the *Independent*,' James remembered. 'One of them ended up a famous man in his own right, he was the one who drove The Beatles from the back of the Adelphi! They didn't know how they were going to get them out. And he went around to the back with the van, and they hopped into the van and they escaped that way.' Sure enough, the newspaper reports confirm The Beatles made their getaway in an *Evening Herald* van, the sister paper of the *Irish Independent*. 'He drove them up to The Gresham,' Frank remembers, 'but the crowd were back there all night waiting for them all to come out of the Adelphi!' It was a good day out for Jack Flanagan, and in any other family perhaps *that* would be the claim to fame.

---

35 Stephen Flaherty, *A Man of No Importance: A New Musical* (Dublin, 2003). 36 Ibid., 77. 37 *The Irish Press*, 14 April 1988.

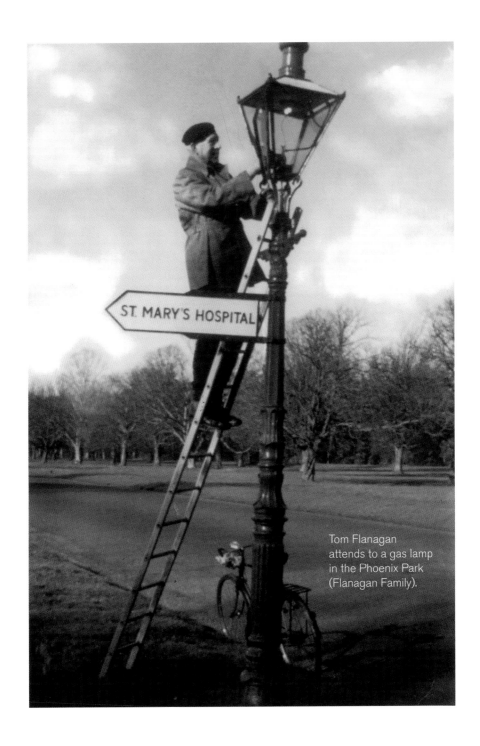

Tom Flanagan
attends to a gas lamp
in the Phoenix Park
(Flanagan Family).

THE LAMPLIGHTERS OF THE PHOENIX PARK

A 1980s image of Tom Flanagan, photographed at the unveiling of refurbished gas lamps on Chesterfield Avenue (Flanagan Family).

Children enjoying a day at Dublin Zoo in the 1950s, from the collections of Fáilte Ireland (Courtesy of Dublin City Library and Archive).

CHAPTER FOUR

Phoenix Park Childhoods

The Phoenix Park is, to some degree, a part of most Dublin childhoods. A visit to the zoo, the Victorian tearooms, and a gander at the deer (but never too close, the sound of clashing antlers ensured that) are all somewhere in my own memory bank of childhood. For the Flanagans however, it was home turf, and the playground of youth. It wasn't that some days were spent in the park – it was a part of their everyday existence and their families' recreational and labouring lives. It is also a place deeply embedded in the wartime memories of Frank Flanagan.

As Frank remembers it, life began 'five doors down from the Hole in the Wall'. For someone who grew up just a few metres from the park at 5 Elm Grove Cottages, he hasn't gone too far. From his home at St Martin's Grove on Blackhorse Avenue today, you can see into the park from the upper floor. It's hard to imagine him living anywhere else.

Frank was born in 1931, at the outset of a decade that would bring enormous changes for the Phoenix Park. In the days of the Emergency, as the period of the Second World War was known in Ireland, Chesterfield Avenue became 'the New Bog Road'. Turf was stacked high, in mounds of up to thirty feet, as a nation wondered if the continental conflict would arrive here. The war colours Frank's recollections of childhood. Sometimes, there are stories of camaraderie and community, but there are also stories of fear. A bomb falling in an English or German city was a news story, as far as the censored media reported it. A bomb falling in the Phoenix Park, as occurred, was a more frightening reality.

James Flanagan was born later, in 1944. These thirteen years between the brothers are significant, but the war was still on when James entered the world, and it continued to leave its imprint on the park for some time.

Frank's memories of the Phoenix Park begin in a time before the Emergency. 'My earliest memories go back into the thirties,' he says, 'and what was outstanding for me was the motorcar races and the motorcycle races. The big name in the motorcar races was Prince Bira, and the big name in the motorbike races was Stanley Woods.'

The Prince Bira Frank remembers was Birabongse Bhanudej of Siam, an early hero of the sport who delighted spectators everywhere. Bullfights, one contemporary had it, 'are less risky and more spectacular'. But there was plenty of spectacle in Prince Bira, who established the national racing colours of Thailand.

OGDEN'S
CIGARETTES

PHOENIX PARK ROAD RACES (MOTOR-CYCLE), JULY 18

Two sides of a 1930s cigarette card depicting the Phoenix Park motorcycle races (Imperial Publishing Limited).

It was another child of the park – albeit one from a very different world to the Flanagans – who had first suggested motor racing. Kenelm Lee Guinness, a member of the Guinness dynasty who had grown up in Farmleigh House within the grounds of the Phoenix Park, was also one of Ireland's foremost racing drivers. Bob Montgomery, a historian who has done much to shine a light on this curious aspect of Irish racing history, has noted:

Each race would be over 300 miles. The scale of the preparations was almost certainly

MOTOR RACES
1931
A SERIES OF 50

44

Phoenix Park Road Races (Motor-cycle), July 18.

'The Dublin Hundred," the first road race organized by the Dublin Motor-Cycle Club was held in Phœnix Park on July 18th. There were forty-seven starters, and the race was run under handicaps over twenty-four laps of the circuit, making the distance of 100 miles. Only ten machines finished, the winner being V. Manifold (Norton) who completed the distance in 1 hr. 26 mins. 17 secs. J. H. Manders (Rudge) spurted towards the end, and put up a record lap at nearly 78 m.p.h. which took him into second place, G. W. Hurst (Enfield) being third. Manifold also won the Novice Cup.

ISSUED BY
· OGDEN'S ·
Commissioned by Fashoda
Authorised reproduction by Imperial Publishing Ltd. © 1993 Imperial Tobacco Limited. First published 1931 Printed in England

greater than that of any sporting event ever held in Ireland and would not have been possible without the enthusiastic support of the government. There was one problem in particular that had to be overcome before the races could take place – the Phoenix Column was situated right bang in the middle of Chesterfield Avenue, on what would be the main straight of the circuit.[1]

The government of the day facilitated this, moving the monument to a site adjacent to the gates of Áras an Uachtaráin. For Frank, there was a certain magic in those days of Prince Bira. We get a sense of that stardom in this 1936 newspaper report:

Thousands thrilled as 'Bira' lapped at an average speed of 99.34 miles an hour, and won the distinction of being the first man to go round the course at more than 100 m.p.h. There was no official estimate of the crowd that lined the course, but everyone was agreed that it was the biggest that ever came to watch a motor race in the Free State.

Motor racing was an occasional spectacle, but a dangerous one. *The Irish Press* complained in 1936 of how a meeting 'was marred by the action of some hundreds of spectators, who refused to remain at the side of the course. Despite the efforts of marshals and police, they crossed the course while the junior race was in progress, to the great danger of themselves and the drivers.'[2]

The main form of racing that brought people to the Phoenix Park was the old Irish reliable, horse racing. Frank remembers that 'from the time I was eleven years of age, I was at the races in the park'. With ease he recalls names like The Mole, Stargazer, and how 'it was a great

---

1 *The Irish Times*, 5 November 2019. See Bob Montgomery, *The Irish International Grand Prix 1929–1931* (Dublin, 2019). 2 *The Irish Press*, 18 September 1933.

Racing in the Phoenix Park (Courtesy of National Library of Ireland).

sprint track'. While James had no interest in horse racing as a sport, he had plenty of interest in the Phoenix Park racecourse, remembering how as kids:

> We'd go in after the races. We'd pick up all the bet tickets. You'd get winners, where people had thrown away the ticket, thinking the horse had been beaten. Or maybe it had come second, but you'd still get something. Particularly if there was an objection, and they wouldn't realise they'd thrown the winning ticket away!

The Phoenix Park racecourse, sitting on the northern edge of the park, was a hive of activity from its opening in 1902. Its presence directly impacted on the park in a broader sense, with trainers availing of a gallop across the Fifteen Acres to train the horses. The intimacy of the venue (to quote one journalist, 'it was a short journey from

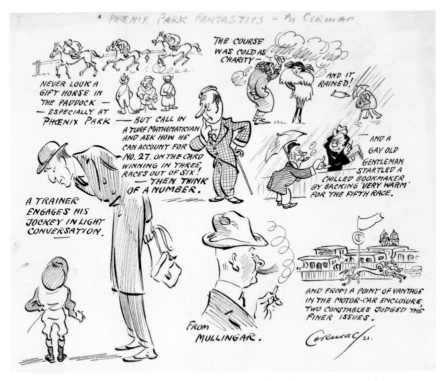

This Ernest Forbes cartoon draws attention to some of the characters one might encounter at the Phoenix Park Racecourse (Courtesy of National Library of Ireland).

gate to paddock, from paddock to bookmaker, from bookmaker to the stand') made it a favourite among Irish racing enthusiasts. Today, apartments with the name Phoenix Park Racecourse, sitting beside the Ashtown Gate, are the only clue to its once thriving existence.

While thousands of Dublin kids might descend on the Phoenix Park on race days, they didn't share the Flanagans' intimate knowledge of the place. For Frank and others raised literally at the wall of the park, they prided themselves on their knowledge of all within it:

> I remember being up in the park gathering sticks to bring home for the fire. And the famous orchards in the park – which we raided! One at what's now the Heritage Centre, where we

The Phoenix Park Racecourse, 1983
(Courtesy of Dublin City Library and Archive).

had our choice of pears and plums and even figs ... We took them, and became professional at it! And other times, if other kids were coming out from town and wondering where the orchards were, we'd tell them where they were. Some of the more ruffian crowd of ours would take the apples off them when they were coming home!

Frank's recollections of the Second World War are vivid, and to his mind, the conflict 'saw the ruin of the Phoenix Park'. As supplies of coal from Britain fell sharply, there was increased emphasis on the need for self-sufficiency, and the Phoenix Park was looked on as a resource that could be used not merely for the storing of turf, but the development of allotments. What was happening beyond Ireland was little understood given the wartime censorship. Indeed, the Irish public had scant knowledge of the diplomatic war of sorts that was being fought within the walls of the Phoenix Park, as the American ambassador David Gray grew increasingly hostile to the Irish position, writing to de Valera that 'Ireland does not seem to appreciate what the war means, the gravity of the situation and the danger of rocking the boat at such a time'.[3] These were nonetheless more considerate words than those of the British ambassador, who reported to London that 'Éire is a bog with a petty leader raking over old muck-heaps.'[4] What the American ambassador could see from his office, in comparison to Britain's John Maffey, was a literal bog.

The historian F.S.L. Lyons famously recalled of the days of neutrality and censorship:

> The tensions – and the liberations – of war, the shared experience, the comradeship in suffering, the new thinking about the future, all these things had passed her [Ireland] by. It was as if an entire people had been condemned to live in Plato's cave, backs to the fire of life and deriving their only knowledge of what went on outside from the flickering shadows thrown on the wall before their eyes by the men and women who passed to and fro behind them. When after six years they emerged, dazzled, from the cave into the light of day, it was to a new and vastly different world.[5]

Lyons may have been correct about the absence of information, but as for the 'shared experience, the comradeship in suffering', there was plenty of that in neutral Éire, including around the Phoenix Park. Frank recalls the presence of allotments in the park, and how his father and other local men – raised and living in an environment different from the tenement landscape of the city – helped families with little experience of the land to grow and harvest food. 'Many of them had never had to do something like that before,' he remembers. 'Fellas from just beyond even Oxmantown Road, they hadn't a clue!'

---

3 Quoted in Conor O'Clery (ed.), *Phrases Make History Here: Political Quotations on Ireland 1886–1987* (Dublin, 1987), 105. 4 Ibid., 102. 5 Quoted in Guy Woodward, *Culture, Northern Ireland, and the Second World War* (Oxford, 2015), 112.

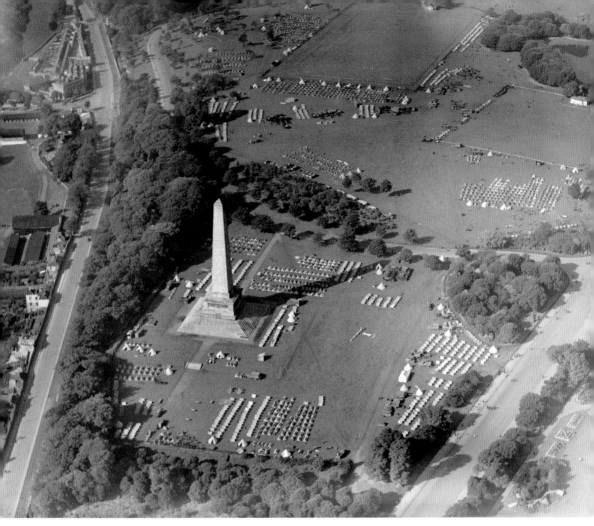

Aerial image of the Phoenix Park from during the Second World War. The park was home to bivouac accommodation for Irish soldiers (Military Archives).

That sense of the ruralness of a place just a few short miles from the city would emerge several times in the memories of both brothers.

Capturing the difficulties of life in wartime, historian Clair Wills has written of how 'the Long Straight [another name for Chesterfield Avenue] in Dublin's Phoenix Park was used for storing huge mountains of turf, and was renamed the New Bog Road'. Chesterfield Avenue, the gaslit jewel of the park, now appeared very different. Wills notes that 'unprocessed turf was hard to burn (a poor-quality sod could be nine-tenths water) and it gave off little heat. Lack of oil and paraffin, in a country where most households still had no electricity supply, was also a great burden.'[6] In time, timber supplies joined the turf. 'The whole park was really covered with fuel dumps or allotments,' Frank remembers, 'but there was very little pilferage. It was the wartime spirit.'

Wartime spirit could only get people so far though, and at remarkably slow speed. With trains fuelled by wood and turf, railway service slowed down to an unimaginable level. In the winter of 1942, Ian Wood writes in his social history of wartime Ireland: 'The 200 mile journey from Killarney to Dublin took 23 hours. One Dublin train travelling to Athlone along a line which ran parallel for some distance to the Royal Canal was passed twice by a barge.'[7] As ever, the satirical Dublin magazine *Dublin Opinion* found humour in the situation. A cartoon depicted a moustached villain, and a lady being tied to a railway line. The caption? 'You can't leave me here, you beast – I'll starve!'[8] The mountains of turf and timber that youngsters like Frank Flanagan looked at in amazement, or climbed up in bravado, were vital to keeping Ireland on the move.

The hardship of life was made worse by the outbreak of foot-and-mouth disease in 1941, which led to the closure of the nearby Dublin Cattle Market for a number of months. Inside the Dáil, the minister for agriculture noted that 'the Dublin area with its dense stock of dairy cattle is regarded as the most dangerous centre'.[9] Right beside the Flanagan family home, on land adjacent to the Hole in the Wall, Frank recalled how the authorities simply dug 'a big long pit, about a hundred and fifty yards long … the army were shooting cows, who were brought to the edge of the pit and shot'. It was just another curious feature of a new reality local children had to adjust to.

Bombs fell on Dublin on several occasions during the war. The city was aware of the devastation caused just hours away, where Luftwaffe

---

6 Clair Wills, *That Neutral Island: A History of Ireland During the Second World War* (London, 2007), 239.
7 Ian S. Wood, *Ireland During the Second World War* (London, 2002), 81. **8** Ibid., 226. **9** Dáil Éireann debates, 23 April 1941 (Houses of the Oireachtas. Volume 82, Number 12).

A 1941 newspaper reporting on one of several occasions when bombs fell on the Irish capital (Courtesy of National Library of Ireland).

raids had claimed the lives of more than 1,100 people in Belfast, and damaged over 56,000 houses in the city. Dublin firefighters had been rushed north on that occasion, a heroic example of assistance in a time of extreme diplomatic tension between Stormont and the Dáil. Perhaps the recollections of Dublin Fire Brigade district officer Michael Rogers are telling of the feeling in the city more broadly: 'It all seemed very remote to me. I looked on it as a deadly game being played in different fields and followed it with a fascinated curiosity.'[10] Yet all changed after the bombing of Belfast, and Dubliners slept a little less soundly. When bombs did fall on the capital, Dublin humour still came through in the darkest of moments: 'At least the Germans know it's the one country … giving Dublin the same as Belfast.'[11]

In the early hours of 31 May 1941, Frank Flanagan and his family were woken by a terrifying sound. A bomb had hit the Phoenix Park. Across the city, other families had a similar experience. The *Sunday Independent* of the following day paints a picture of a city in a state of intense panic:

> Planes had been heard over the city from shortly after midnight, and anti-aircraft defences and searchlights immediately went into action. Long eerie fingers of light from the searchlights swept backward and forwards searching for the planes, and anti-aircraft shells could be seen bursting in the clear sky …
>
> Heartrending scenes were witnessed at the North Strand as dead, dying and seriously injured people were brought out of their ruined homes. Children ran screaming through the streets in their night attire and were cared for by people in the neighbourhood whose houses had been less seriously injured.[12]

The paper reported how the final bomb 'fell in the Phoenix Park beside the pumping station at the Dog Pond. One house was badly damaged, but there were only two casualties – a man and his daughter – who were slightly injured.'[13] Frank remembers the shock on visiting the park the next day, and discovering the remnants of the bombing:

> When the bomb fell, it blew all the windows out of Áras an Uachtaráin. We went in to see it the next morning. There was

---

10 Donal Fallon, 'When Dublin Responded to Blitzed Belfast's May-day', *History Ireland* (Volume 19, Issue 3). 11 J.A. O'Brien, *Against the Wind: Memoir of a Dissident Dubliner* (Victoria, 2013). 12 *Sunday Independent*, 1 June 1941. 13 Ibid.

THE LAMPLIGHTERS OF THE PHOENIX PARK

a tree about fifteen feet from where the big hole was – the tree had all the skin gone off it and all the leaves. My cousin Nicky got a bit of the bomb stuck in one of the trees, got it out and took it home. A jagged piece of metal.

But Joe McNally's house was only twenty yards from the bomb site, and he was there with his daughter. And their house collapsed … None of them were hurt, but the young one shouted, 'Daddy, I feel something's on top of me.' It was the rafters of the house. But he got her out, and they were only yards from where the bomb was.

Frank talks movingly of the experience of that night, and how it brought neighbours together. Those who were frightened sought comfort and solace in the homes of others:

I will never forget it … my father put us all under the bed, it was a big double bed in the back room, and he stood at the window and was watching out. I remember my mother telling him to get away from the window, the windows will break in. There was Matt Reid, two doors up who was afraid of his life, and he came in to us and he was also in the back room. My father said half of Dublin is after being bombed.

For families living in and around different areas of the park, the war posed varying threats to livelihoods. Michael Ward, then a youngster living in Society House in the zoo with his grandfather, recalled how his relation, the chief superintendent of the zoo, rushed out with a gun in hand after hearing the same blast as the Flanagans, fearful of escaped animals:

He was only worried about the wolves because they're scavengers and would vanish quickly. Lions and leopards would make for the open. But all was in good order. Not a

An aerial view of Áras an Uachtaráin, from the papers of President Seán T. O'Kelly (Courtesy of National Library of Ireland)..

pane of glass was broken in the Lion House. Next day, my grandfather noticed that the bison had charged the railings but not broken through. And Sarah [the elephant] had opened her door, gone down to the lake, and then returned to her house. We found her footprints and noticed that her door was open.[14]

A bomb falling next to your home has the effect of focusing the mind, Frank recounting that: 'We had gas masks; we never had to use them, but there was one for every member of a household. Before the bombing we only used them for playing and scaring one another.'

---

14 Catherine de Courcy, *Dublin Zoo: An Illustrated History* (Cork, 2009), 139.

Another resident near the bomb site, President Douglas Hyde, felt the same blast as the Flanagan family. A secret Áras an Uachtaráin report noted how 'one of the windows of the President's bedroom in which he was at the time sleeping was broken and a portion of the mantelpiece was dislodged'.[15] Historian Brian Murphy has written of how 'at the outbreak of the war, an outdoor coal cellar in the grounds of Áras an Uachtaráin had been converted into a temporary, if amateur-style, air-raid shelter by reinforcing it with 200 sandbags'.[16] Hyde, then in his eighties, remained in the park throughout the war years.

'And then,' Frank remembers, 'the park went dark.' In the aftermath of the bombing, the three significant residencies there all requested a blackout, removing a ritual from the life of their father and greatly decreasing any activity in the park after dark. It added to the sense of eeriness of the time.

Frank also remembers another aspect of the war clearly, and how something as simple and fundamentally Irish as a cup of tea became a luxury. 'Things were rationed, and people were issued with ration books. We were very well off in that regard because with seven or eight kids at the time our house got nearly a pound of tea.' There was even 'black market tea', and Frank remembers neighbours asking him to try to procure some from the area around the school. At the time, Ireland had the second-highest consumers of tea in the world. A British servicewoman stationed in Northern Ireland wrote of a visit to Dublin:

> Tea is the only thing the people are really desperate about, and you can exchange it for practically anything, so we had taken as much as we could get hold of. The tea ration in Éire has been reduced to ½ oz a week for each person, so you can

---

15 *Irish Independent*, 31 May 2016. 16 See Brian Murphy, *Forgotten Patriot: Douglas Hyde and the Foundation of the Irish Presidency* (Dublin, 2016).

understand their desperation. Most of the restaurants will only serve tea at certain times.[17]

The struggle for tea inspired children's street rhymes across the country, rhymes that even decades later are still easily recalled by men and women of Frank's generation. One that was widely heard in Dublin and other urban centres named the politicians of the day:

> *Bless them all, bless them all*
> *The long and the short and the tall*
> *Bless de Valera, and Seán McEntee*
> *Who gave us brown bread, and a half-ounce of tea*
> *And they rationed the cocoa and all*
> *And sure it needn't be rationed at all.*
> *They're bringing starvation, to our destination*
> *Thank God for St Vincent de Paul!*[18]

Rationing extended to gas too, and the much-feared 'glimmer man' was tasked with ensuring households were not using gas outside permitted hours or too liberally. This was, to quote historian Bryce Evans, seen as 'the embodiment of Emergency petty officialdom'.[19] When writer Roddy Doyle interviewed his mother on the matter, she recalled the great sense of guilt her family felt about using gas out of hours, and how 'it was all very surreptitiously done; we were put to the front door, on sentry duty, to make sure the glimmer man wasn't coming'.[20]

Some impacts of wartime are more surprising. As petrol was rationed, and private car use was essentially prohibited for large

---

17 Wills, *That Neutral Island*, 240.   **18** This is just one variation of this popular street rhyme. For an interesting discussion, see the Mudcat lyrical forum. https://mudcat.org/thread.cfm?threadid=95663 (Accessed February 2023).   **19** Bryce Evans, *Ireland during the Second World War: Farewell to Plato's Cave* (Manchester, 2014).   **20** Roddy Doyle, *Rory and Ita* (Dublin, 2008), 131.

periods of time with only special exceptions; this meant the return of the Dublin jarvey in a big way. These men were perfectly described by oral historian Kevin C. Kearns, who met a number of them in his field research:

> Proud and competitive, they drove the streets perched atop their jaunting cars or five-wheeled carriages drawn by often magnificently groomed horses with brass and leather gleaming. They did grand horse funerals, took spectators out to the races, and frequented the bonafides for midnight pints.[21]

A bonafide was a public house that could serve certain customers after closing hours in the city, provided they were far enough from home. Stout seemed one of the few goods still available to the same standard as before. Describing the scene in Dublin, British press attaché John Betjeman wrote of how there was 'no petrol, no light, no coal, no trains', but there remained Guinness.[22] An all-important detail.

Frank still recalls the 'Song of the Dublin Jarvey', which alluded to several local landmarks:

> *If you want to drive round Dublin*
> *Sure you'll find me on the stand*
> *I'll take you to Raheny*
> *For cockles on the strand*
> *To Phoenix Park, to Nancy Hands*
> *To the monument and then*
> *I'll take you to the Strawberry Beds*
> *And back to town again.*

---

21 Kearns, *Dublin Street Life and Lore*, 48.   22 Antoinette Quinn, *Patrick Kavanagh: A Biography* (Dublin, 2001), 166.

Frank and James Flanagan at the Hole in the Wall, previously called Nancy Hands (Luke Fallon).

Nancy Hands, not to be confused with the pub of that name on Parkgate Street today, was an earlier trading name for the Hole in the Wall. Against the backdrop of limited car transportation, the jarvey became a familiar sight once again. Recalling what was on the road in the war years, Peter Somerville-Large writes of 'broughams, hansom cabs, landaus and brakes ... pulled out of sheds and once more took their place on the road'. Dublin, it seemed, 'reverted to the past'.[23] Jarveys and sidecars brought visitors to places like the Hole in the Wall, and there was work (a rare thing against the political and economic backdrop of the day) for local kids in providing a waiting service outside the premises. As Frank recalls:

> I was lucky enough one day I was on my own – and up came a sidecar with four or six on it, and I got the job of minding the horses ... the next thing, a disaster. My father came up on his bike with the ladder behind him. 'What's this scrounging and begging! Get the hell out of it!' I had to let go, my friend Paddy took the job and he got six pence – and I missed out on that.

James, too young to have the same recollections of wartime, still remembers the aftermath of the war, and the physical imprint left on the park. 'Where the pope's cross is at the moment, that was all full of coal. I spent my early summer holidays there digging up coal from the ground that was left over. The coal had been there for such a time it had actually gone into the ground. We all got loads of coal out of it when it was finished.'

The Second World War may have been known by another name here, but it required much of the same spirit and will as was found elsewhere. The writer Elizabeth Bowen, reporting on the conditions

---

23 Peter Somerville-Large, *Dublin: The Fair City* (London, 1996), 262.

in Ireland to the Foreign Office in London , insisted that that 'at present Éire suffers in all senses, and while her deprivations are far less than Britain's, they have to be met without the heroic stimulus that comes from participation in the war'.[24] One doesn't have to fight in a war to experience its effects.

In the years of the Emergency, even the festive season suffered. 'Christmas 1941 was a bleak one,' Frank remembers. 'Most of the men were either in England, unemployed or in the army.' Despite Ireland's military neutrality, there was no ban on Irish people travelling to Britain to assist in the war effort, and many worked in munitions factories or helped keep British cities functioning against the backdrop of the Blitz. Times were tighter during the war, but there were also moments of great community resilience. That same year, Frank asked a neighbour what Santa had brought him, only to be told, 'Nothing, he never came to our house.' Another neighbour then intervened:

> 'Tell them to come here,' Mrs O'Neill said. They came down and she brought out a big brown bag with number seven on it and full of toys. She said, 'That oul' Santa, he does be drunk at Christmas, he left that bag in my house. He should have known that I have no children and should have left it in number seven instead of my place.'

This was, to Frank's memory, 'an act of decency in the rare old times'. Mrs O'Neill had saved Christmas for one family, an act of generosity remembered even now, eight decades on.

After the years of the Emergency passed, a more normal childhood returned. The wartime president, Douglas Hyde, became a figure of curiosity to a young Frank, who briefly had a job working in what is now known as Ratra House. Wheelchair-bound following a stroke,

---

24 Wills, *That Neutral Island*, 249.

President Douglas Hyde, as drawn by the cartoonist and political activist Grace Gifford-Plunkett (Courtesy of National Library of Ireland).

and retired from the office of president, Hyde lived in a building that was originally known as Little Lodge, but which he christened Teach Ráth an tSratha – or Ratra House – in honour of his country residence in Roscommon. Located next door to the Áras, it had once been the official residence of the private secretary to the lord lieutenant of Ireland. 'When I was working in the garden, which was a great little job to land in the summer for a local lad, I'd sometimes see him wheeled around.' Hyde was so weakened in the later years of his life that when the prestigious artist Seán O'Sullivan painted him in 1944, Hyde sat for head and shoulders only. He relied on his aide-de-camp, Éamon de Buitléar, to serve as a model for the standing figure.

James has very different first memories of the park to Frank. 'Football is my main one,' he says. 'At the Hole in the Wall, we had a kind of pitch that we made up ourselves, and every day from spring right through to October we played football. And the Furry Glen, we used to go over there with dogs and hunt rabbits – it was a great place for kids just poking around.' Amidst the strange reminders there had just been a global war, and how the park played its part in the Irish response to it, kids got back to the business of playing.

There were times when the entire city seemed to descend on the park, like the weekly performances in the Hollow and at the bandstand near the zoo, with both brothers recalling these concerts with great fondness. This was a tradition that stretched back to a much earlier time, one of 'ladies linking arms with mustachioed dandies, bare-footed street urchins from the tenements and the old fruit sellers who benefited from the passing trade'.[25] A guidebook to the park from decades past speaks of 'the famous St James's Brass and Reed Band, the York Street Band, later known as Ireland's Own, and the Wellington Quay Band'. Still, the most peculiar band to have played the Hollow in its heyday came from one unique band of youngsters. A guidebooks tells us:

> Of particular note was the Glencree Reformatory Band. Its
> members were placed under heavy police escort at the Hollow,

---

25 Barry Kennerk, *The Peeler's Notebook: Policing Victorian Dublin* – Mad Dogs, Duals and Dynamite (Dublin, 2019).

A view of the famous Phoenix Park Hollow and bandstand (Courtesy of National Library of Ireland).

in case anyone was tempted to make a dash for freedom. Yes, though the young musicians were banded as criminals their music was greatly appreciated. On one occasion they astounded their audience with a magnificent performance of the 1812 Overture, a major undertaking for a junior band.[26]

Those glory days of the Hollow, which remains a popular spot close to the zoo, predated the Flanagans. Gone were the men of the Dublin

---

26 Kenneth MacGowan, *The Phoenix Park: Dramatic Story of Ireland's Great Park* (Dublin, 1960), 30.

The Cattle Market, from the Robert French Collection. A vitally important part of the local economy which lent Stoneybatter the name 'Cowtown' (Courtesy of National Library of Ireland).

Metropolitan Police and Royal Irish Constabulary bands, replaced instead by the Garda Band. 'I remember our mother would pay for the foldable seats, it was a great place which had its own atmosphere,' Frank recalls, and how the amphitheatre of the Hollow provided a great escape from the city beyond.

For James and Frank, there was a feeling that they were growing up in an area that was part of Dublin and yet slightly removed from it. Walking down Blackhorse Avenue, they knew they were close to 'Cowtown', the colloquial name bestowed on Stoneybatter and its surroundings, owing to the presence of the Dublin Cattle Market. 'We fed into Cowtown,' Frank remembers, and the brothers' recollections recalled for me the picture painted by journalist Gene Kerrigan, who grew up nearby in 1950s Cabra:

> The cattle were tended by cowboys on bicycles, men with overcoats and hats, furiously pedalling this way and that, whacking the cattle with their sticks and shouting at them, the bewildered beasts leaving heaps of shit on the road as souvenirs of their passage.[27]

James too remembers the evidence the cows left behind, and the sounds as they made their way down Blackhorse Avenue. A road with a long military tradition, familiar to the sound of marching men, this particular ritual had echoes of a formation on the move:

> It was amazing on a Wednesday morning – market morning. I'd wake up at two or three in the morning, you'd hear the whistling of the fellas coming down driving the cows. You could hear the sticks hopping off the wall and fellas roaring. You'd go down the next morning and you couldn't stand with the cow dung on the road.

Both brothers attended schools nearer to the city, in Frank's case the Christian Brothers School on North Brunswick Street. On the day we were driving through the park, taking pictures for this book, we passed the old Phoenix Park School. 'We were in there for a bit,' Frank remembered, 'and most of the local kids went to school there. But the idea of a Protestant teacher teaching the kids Holy Communion was too much! When my mother brought me down to the other school the nuns said there was no room, but they changed their mind quickly when they heard the story! Come in! Come in!'

---

27 Gene Kerrigan, *Another Country: Growing Up In '50s Ireland – Memoirs of a Dublin Childhood* (Dublin, 1998)

His teacher was the famous Paddy Crosbie, a broadcaster best remembered for *The School around the Corner*, a popular radio programme which later made the leap to television. A copy of Paddy's best-selling book *Your Dinner's Poured Out* is signed 'To Frank, one of the Brunner Boys'. Frank remembers schooldays with Crosbie fondly:

> He encouraged pupils to bring in a kind of news report of events that took place after or before school. One lad had a report that said, 'When I was going home from school yesterday, a horse and cart fell into a hole in the road. The horse broke his leg so they shot him.' 'In the hole?', asked Crosbie. 'No, in the head,' came the reply.

It was a school with a long working-class pedigree, Crosbie remembering how 'when Brunner opened its doors first in February 1869, according to the annals, practically all of the boys who turned up to be enrolled were barefooted'. A former pupil himself, he recalled how the students were raised on a diet of nationalist heroics:

> *When the Brother teaches History*
> *Each week he picks one day.*
> *We fold our arms an' sit up straight*
> *Our books is pur' away*
> *We listen very quietly*
> *To the stories he does tell,*
> *An' everytime the Irish win,*
> *We all ler' out a yell.*[28]

The children in North Brunswick Street came, by and large, from a different world to that of the Flanagans, who had the open

---

28 Paddy Crosbie, *Your Dinner's Poured Out!* (Dublin, 1981), 185–6.

expanses of the Phoenix Park on their doorstep. Frank remembers the tenement homes of many, where there were 'always so many prams at the bottoms of the stairs'. Many of the other students had no familiarity at all with the park, or the vast open spaces it offered. Sometimes, the other students regarded him as almost from the country:

> I remember swapping a cattle stick for a pocket dictionary with one of the lads in school. You'd get sixpence for bringing up four or five cattle ... and you were lucky if you got a bull, because you got a shilling for bringing up a bull ... Then it became a racket, with a number of them missing out of school on a Wednesday. Paddy Crosbie was the teacher, and he lived up on Glenbeigh Road. He went home for his dinner one Wednesday to Glenbeigh Road, but he got down off the bike and he went into the cattle market, and there's seven or eight of them that was missing out of the class all against the wall with their cattle sticks. So he took one fella's stick and drove them down the road like a herd of cattle!

James had a similar experience, though it was also different in a way, recalling how, 'I went to St Gabriel's School in Oxmantown Road. O'Devaney Gardens were the main people who went there, so I was called a culchie when I went there! But the North Circular Road was kind of the junction, to many, that was where town ended.'

O'Devaney Gardens, from which most of James's classmates came, was an extraordinary development in public housing, in terms of scale. It consisted of thirteen four-storey blocks, 'set mostly in parallel rows on a twelve-acre field'. Yet as architectural historian Ellen Rowley notes, this massive development was, in other ways, almost invisible and set apart: 'The complex of blocks was cut off from its Edwardian neighbourhood, barely visible from the North Circular Road, and in its invisibility it could become a disconnected domain of its own.'[29] It is difficult to imagine a place less like Blackhorse Avenue, though the park gates were also mere minutes walk from O'Devaney Gardens.'

In the community that James and Frank grew up in, there were some traditions that were virtually unknown to their respective classmates. Frank remembers 'wren day', which is still observed in parts of Ireland annually on St Stephen's Day, also known as *Lá an Dreoilín* (the day of the wren). It was an integral part of the magic of Christmas, a time of year that provided some financial opportunities:

> We searched for berried holly in the woods beforehand and sold it door to door. Nearer to Christmas we would make the trip to the west end of the park, the Furry Glen, where we would procure a large bush for wren day. We would try to trap a wren – normally, no luck!

The day consisted – and still consists – of 'strawboys' in costume seeking out a wren bird, before parading through streets and seeking hospitality from households in the area. With ease, he recited the traditional song of the 'wren boys', going from house to house on the day:

> *The wren, the wren, the king of all birds,*
> *St Stephen's Day was caught in the furze,*
> *Although he was little his honour was great,*
> *Jump up me lads and give him a treat.*
>
> *Up with the kettle and down with the pan,*
> *And give us a penny to bury the wren.*

---

29 Ellen Rowley, *Housing, Architecture and the Edge Condition: Dublin Is Building, 1935–1975* (Oxfordshire, 2020).

The residence
of the American
Ambassador
(Luke Fallon).

Not alone did their neighbours not know the lads were coming
door to door, but Frank recalls how 'the older lads went to the US
ambassador's residence with the wren bush'. As peculiar as the
tradition might have been to people in other parts of Dublin, imagine
the surprise of the staff of the ambassador's Deerfield Residence,
formerly the Chief Secretary's Lodge. But to the youngsters engaging
in the annual tradition, it was just another neighbour to call on.

While it was great fun for his friends, Frank knew that this custom was totally alien to most of the students in the 'Brunner':

> This was like a village outside town. None of the kids in town went around with the wren bush; when I went to school in town, the kids didn't know what I was talking about. This was like a rural thing, going around with the wren bush and getting treated at each house.

Even when Frank and James have memories of childhood that have a Dublin universality about them, the park adds a new dimension to their telling. The cinema has long been a feature of any Dublin memoir, and Paddy Crosbie rattled them off like old friends:

> There was the 'Manor' or 'Broadway' on Manor Street, the 'Tivo' in Francis Street, the 'Roto', i.e. the Rotunda downtown, the 'Fizzer' at Blaquiere, the 'Fountain' in James's Street, the 'Eleck' in Talbot Street. Last, but not least, the 'Feeno', i.e. The Phoenix Picture Palace on Ellis Quay.[30]

James remembers how 'we went to Chapelizod to the Oriel, which was up behind the Mullingar House pub. Every Sunday night we'd go on the bikes, with a race across the park. The minute it was over they'd be set up, and there'd be a race back home.' From one parkside community to another, the image of these children racing across a park they knew so well is perhaps only matched by Frank's recollections of children arriving on horseback to a cinema showing a tale of cowboys and Indians.

Surprisingly, for a place that was just the other side of the Phoenix Park, Chapelizod was mostly alien territory to the Flanagans. With its deep connections to the writer Sheridan Le Fanu, who set his classic

---

30 Crosbie, *Your Dinner's Poured Out!*, 119.

The House by the Churchyard (1863) there, Chapelizod had its own traditions and stories.[31] Its children sought out different ghosts, and knew different park gates, but had their own obsessions and fascination with the park. Indeed, Chapelizod itself felt like a totally different place, further removed from the city than even the still rural-feeling Blackhorse Avenue, something Joyce had captured in *Dubliners*: 'Mr James Duffy,' he told us, 'lived in Chapelizod because he wished to live as far as possible from the city of which he was a citizen and because he found all the other suburbs of Dublin mean, modern and pretentious.'[32]

The great Dublin song collector and singer Frank Harte, raised in Chapelizod, would record and collect many songs which documented the Phoenix Park and its historic journey.[33] These places, while close in some ways and with common historical traits, were also distinctive. Chapelizod was shaped by its proximity to the Liffey, while the families of Blackhorse Avenue instead knew things like the cattle market.

Cattle marching past to the market weren't the only animals that were part of the Flanagan childhood. Within the Phoenix Park too there were animals of all kinds. The deer were always respected. 'We never got as near to them though as the kids do today,' Frank says. 'We wouldn't get within twenty yards or fifty yards of the deer.' The zoo was also part of life for local children, who were often looked to for assistance. Frank remembers how 'a number of us got jobs in the zoo, looking after pony rides. If you got a job in there you got two bob for the afternoon, bringing the horses up and down with kids on them.' James remembers how the local area could give kids an 'in' to the zoo, and how he knew Bob O'Neill, a bird keeper:

> He brought me down; I was absolutely amazed by the animals that were there and spent most of my day with the lions. I

---

31 See Motoko Fujita, *The Shadow of James Joyce: Chapelizod and Environs* (Dublin, 2011). 32 James Joyce, *Dubliners* (London, 1914), 133. 33 See Terry Moylan (ed.), *A Living Voice: The Frank Harte Song Collection* (Dublin, 2020).

remember one time bringing my sister down, it was dark, and lucky enough my father, coming up on his bike and who caught the two of us heading towards the zoo, put us on the handlebar and brought us home.

That a child like James, born in the first half of the 1940s, would be fascinated by Dublin Zoo isn't surprising. It was making a real impression as the decade concluded. 'Clicking merrily throughout the summer,' readers of the *Irish Independent* were told in September 1949, 'the turnstiles of the Zoological Gardens admitted more visitors than ever before in the peak month of August.'[34] Crowds flocked to see a famous lion of the big screen, and the world of MGM:

> Each day recently, the lion house was crowded when Mr C.L. Flood, Superintendent, visited his charges ... In the next cage, Stephen, now the most widely known 'tough guy' of the screen, paced up and down registering royalty and majesty for all he was worth. He cannot forget that two years ago, when Metro-Goldwyn-Mayer's original roaring lion film became worn out, he was chosen from all the lions in the world for the star role. Stephen was 'a natural', obedient to Mr Flood's quiet orders he turned his head to just the right angle and roared at exactly the right moment. Since then, he is the first star to appear in every MGM film on every screen in the world.[35]

Within the park, the post-war years saw a relaxation around places that had been caught up in the earlier excitement. The American ambassador's residence, from which David Gray had fired such sharp political arrows in the direction of government during the war,

---

34 *Irish Independent*, 2 September 1949. **35** Ibid.

questioning Irish neutrality, was now a more relaxed place. 'I palled around with a mate of mine, Billy McDonald,' James says. 'I spent most of my days in there with him. His father was working in there ... We'd go fishing for pinkeens around it. We would walk straight through it. By the house, and around the house, and even jumped the wall at the Acres side.' Even the Áras seemed a more relaxed place. An orchard, too good to resist, was easy pickings for James and his friends: 'We did an orchard in there – President O'Kelly came across us, walking the pathway. He said, "How are you, boys?" We kind of said, "We're grand, howaya!" Not realising who it was at the time.'

These are the kinds of stories very few Dublin children could tell, of casual encounters with the president or jumping the wall of the American ambassador's residence. The author Máirín Johnston, born in Dublin's Liberties in the same year as Frank Flanagan, reflected on her own working-class Dublin childhood:

> For these children, childhood was all work and no play, but most of us did have one freedom – the freedom of the streets. This was the only place we could be ourselves, free from the restrictions of the adult world. Here we could make our own rules, elect our own leaders and impose our own code of values. Playing on the streets gave us our only space to develop our imaginations and our individual personalities.[36]

For the Flanagan boys, the freedom of the streets was matched by the freedom of the park.

---

36 Máirín Johnson, 'Dublin Childhoods', in *Growing Up Poor*, published by Galway Labour History Group (Galway, 1993).

A postcard image of Lord Gough's statue. While the quality of Foley's work was undeniable, the monument was targeted on a number of occasions (Courtesy of Dublin City Library and Archive).

CHAPTER FIVE

From Gough to the 'Fenian's Bark'

There was the man in the grey suit, walking up the middle of the road, always with a paper under his arm in the night time. He never answered when anyone said hello to him. It was reckoned that was Burke.

There was the famous one, down at the cricket grounds, of a horseman with a head under his arms. We always swore that must have been Gough!

Cross marking the location of the 1882 Phoenix Park assassinations (Luke Fallon).

For Frank Flanagan, like all children who grew up around the park, it was a place of ghost stories. Maureen Grant from nearby Queen Street, a fondly remembered Dublin character who ran the bar of Dublin's Olympia Theatre for many decades, recalled mitching from school in the Phoenix Park. She remembered the fright of encountering 'the banshee' of the park, and how 'I ran all the way home into Queen Street'.[1] The ghosts that Frank recalls owed less to the supernatural world and more to the history of the Phoenix Park itself. The Burke he speaks of was Thomas Henry Burke, permanent under-secretary, who was assassinated by political opponents as he walked in the park in May 1882, alongside Frederick Cavendish, the recently appointed chief secretary of Ireland. Cavendish wasn't just new in the job – it was his first day in Dublin. The 'Phoenix Park

1 Kevin C. Kearns, *Stoneybatter: Dublin's Inner-Urban Village* (Dublin, 1996), 150.

THE LAMPLIGHTERS OF THE PHOENIX PARK

Murders', as they were widely labelled in the press, would make the park synonymous with the question of Ireland's place in the empire.

The horseman that Frank and other children swore they would see in the park was presumed to be Field Marshal Hugh Gough, formerly commander-in-chief of India, and commander of the forces that defeated the Sikhs in the 1840s. A statue to Gough was once one of the defining features of the Phoenix Park, unveiled with much military pomp and ceremony in 1878. Though gone more than six decades, many still allude to 'Gough Roundabout', near to the imposing Wellington obelisk. The statue may be gone, but we can still see the brilliant hand of its sculptor in the capital today.

John Henry Foley's work is to be found across the world, but his most famous piece is undoubtedly the fine monument to Daniel O'Connell. Known to Irish history as 'The Liberator', the constitutional nationalist gazes down over the O'Connell Bridge, his monument bearing the scars of the revolutionary period clearly. Bullets, most from Easter week 1916, but perhaps a few from the Battle of Dublin which commenced the Civil War in the summer of 1922, have left their mark in O'Connell's arm, chest and cloak.

Foley may be responsible for this celebrated monument to an Irish nationalist leader, but much of his work commemorated figures of the British empire. Queen Victoria, a great admirer of Foley's style, insisted that he carry out the figure of Prince Albert for the Albert Memorial in London. Born at 6 Montgomery Street (the origin of the name 'Monto') in the heart of working-class Dublin, Foley was buried in the crypt of St Paul's Cathedral in London, a recognition of his importance to his art form. Walter Strickland, the leading authority on nineteenth-century Irish sculpture, insisted that Foley's works 'show a vitality, a knowledge and sense of structure and movement, and a decorative feeling, which were absent in the cold and lifeless works of his contemporaries'.[2]

---

2 Quoted in Judith Hill, *Irish Public Sculpture: A History* (Dublin, 1998), 259.

The works did not all fare as well as O'Connell. For example, there was Lord Dunkellin, who stood in Galway's Eyre Square for almost five decades. When independence came in 1922, local people took it upon themselves to banish Foley's statue. A witness described seeing 'a large mob headed by a man dragging with ropes the statue of Lord Dunkellin from Eyre Square, some sitting on the statue as if they were on a sledge'.[3] Into the River Corrib went Dunkellin, to the sound of a singing crowd, as a band played 'I'm Forever Blowing Bubbles'. Even at the remove of a century, some of Foley's memorials remain controversial. In 2020, and with the emergence of the Black Lives Matter movement, Foley's statue of Confederate General Thomas 'Stonewall' Jackson was removed from public display in the United States. Even at the time of writing this book, there were questions around some of Foley's work. A statue of Prince Albert, husband of Queen Victoria, still stands at the rear of Leinster House. A TD, seeking its removal, commented that 'it seems we are embarrassed enough to let the statue be overgrown by a hedge, but not enough to just remove the statue'.[4]

Chesterfield Avenue is no longer home to a John Henry Foley work, but for many years his statue of Gough was one of the most imposing features of the road, before its removal at the hands of a republican bomb. 'Ireland,' a nineteenth-century critic insisted, 'now can boast of possessing in the Gough memorial the finest equestrian statue in the British Isles'.[5]

The Gough statue is not only a part of the childhood of Frank Flanagan, but also that of Winston Churchill, who attended its unveiling. For a young Churchill, the Phoenix Park was briefly home, when his grandfather served as viceroy and his father worked in the

---

3 Daniel Joseph Murphy, *Lady Gregory's Journals, Volume 14* (Oxford, 1978), 359. 4 Newstalk coverage of comments by Peadar Tóibín, TD: https://www.newstalk.com/podcasts/highlights-from-the-hard-shoulder/quite-incredible-that-prince-albert-statue-remains-at-leinster-house-toibin. 5 *Irish Monthly Magazine* (Volume 9, 1881), 232.

While the focus of this image is 'strollers and cyclists in the Phoenix Park', it gives a sense of the scale of the Gough statue (Courtesy of National Library of Ireland).

Viceregal Lodge alongside him. Churchill would later ask, 'When does one first begin to remember? When do the waving lights and shadows of dawning consciousness cast their print upon the mind of a child? My earliest memories are Ireland.'[6] More specifically, his earliest memory was the unveiling of the statue to Gough:

> A great black crowd, scarlet soldiers on horseback, strings pulling away a brown shiny sheet, the Old Duke, the formidable grandpa, talking loudly to the crowd. I recall even

---

6 Quoted in Thomas and Valeria Pakenham, *Dublin: A Traveller's Reader* (London, 2018), 111.

a phrase he used: 'And with a withering volley he shattered the enemy's line.' I quite understood that he was speaking about war and fighting and that a volley meant what the black-coated soldiers (riflemen) used to do with loud bangs so often in the Phoenix Park where I was taken for morning walks.[7]

From 1878, Gough on horseback greeted all who travelled up Chesterfield Avenue. It, and other imperial monuments, can emerge in the most surprising of Dublin memoirs. Michael Ryan, later a participant in the IRA's border campaign of the 1950s, remembered it as a 'magnificent memorial', and how:

> My father would say 'that's the finest statue of its kind in the world, and it was done by a Dublin man named Foley. That's bronze,' he'd say, and he'd walk us around the statue, examining the beautiful lines of the horse. The proud, seated figure on it and the strength and unity of horse and rider never failed to thrill me and provoke my imagination to thoughts of the battles he fought and to regret that I had never done such things.[8]

Post-independence, it was perhaps unsurprising that he became a target for attack. Frank recalled the excitement amongst local kids, who discovered 'one Christmas Eve in the 1940s, that someone climbed onto Gough's horse and cut the head off the rider'. The head was later discovered in low tide near Islandbridge, gifted to the Liffey by those who had sawn it off. Whatever of a monument being beheaded making for unusual headlines ('the Headless Horseman of the Phoenix Park'), 'Gough To Be Re-Headed' was a curious one too.

---

7 Alfred Leslie Rowse, *The Later Churchills* (London, 1958), 237. **8** Michael Ryan, *My Life in the IRA: The Border Campaign* (Cork, 2018), 30–1.

This image gives a sense of the impressive scale of Foley's work (Courtesy of National Library of Ireland).

In the pages of *The Irish Times*, Myles na gCopaleen (pen-name of the writer Brian O'Nolan) found the entire thing a little ridiculous:

> Few people will sympathise with this activity; some think it is simply wrong, others do not understand how anybody could think of getting up in the middle of a frosty night in order to saw the head off a metal statue …
>
> The Gough statue in question was a monstrosity, famous only for the disproportion of the horse's legs; its present headlessness gives it a grim humour and even if the head is recovered, I urge strongly that no attempt should be made to solder it on.[9]

---

9 Donal Fallon, 'Neath the horse's prick, a dynamite stick', Come Here To Me, 24 January 2012, https://comeheretome.com/2012/01/24/now-he-sits-in-chillingham-castle/.

Gough, recovered head and all, lived to fight another day. In July 1957, an explosion damaged the memorial, leading to its eventual removal. Frank remembers that 'Dubliners were quick with parodies and within days we had a song to the air of "Lili Marlene".'

> *When Nelson heard the story he shouted to Parnell*
> *'How long will I be left here, oh Charlie can you tell?*
> *I don't feel safe upon his seat,*
> *I must retreat down to the street*
> *Like Gough's immortal statue, up near the Magazine.*

Little could Admiral Nelson have known it, but his own impending doom was on the horizon. An explosion on 8 March 1966 removed Nelson Pillar from O'Connell Street, a republican contribution to the golden jubilee of the Easter Rising which sent a number of songs such as The Go Lucky Four's 'Up Went Nelson' to the top of the charts. Just as in the aftermath of the Nelson Pillar blast, the Gough explosion before it offered an opportunity to Dublin wits. A story, almost certainly apocryphal, spread throughout to the city that the taoiseach had received a telegram advising him to back a horse that would be running in the park. This would naturally be taken as a tip for the Phoenix Park racecourse. The next morning, Gough's horse had been displaced.[10]

Frank Flanagan's recitation of 'Gough's Immortal Statue' allowed me to introduce him to another work, written at the time of the attack. A fine piece of verse did the rounds in the public houses of Dublin in the days that followed, and which was wrongly attributed to Brendan Behan. Wisely, Behan never actually denied authoring the work, recognising its lyrical brilliance. It ended:

---

10 Jim Lacey, *The Barony of Castleknock* (Dublin, 2015).

For this is the way,
our 'hayroes' today
Are challenging England's might,
With a stab in the back and a midnight attack
On a statue that can't even ——!

This 'viral' piece of Dublin doggerel was the work of Vincent Caprani, Dublin poet and printer. It was, in his own words, a pop at the 'armchair generals' who had taken aim at a bronze horse.[11]

Dublin was a city that had long prided itself on the ability to respond quickly (and often crudely) to on-going events. Monuments were frequently ridiculed not long after their unveilings, like the statue of Lady Justice within the grounds of Dublin Castle, gazing away from the metropolis and in on the administration. Indeed, the tradition continued through to contemporary interventions in the city like the countdown clock in the Liffey for the millennium ('the time in the slime'), and the Anna Livia fountain on O'Connell Street ('the floozie in the jacuzzi'). Post-independence, Dublin wits were no longer commenting on monuments themselves, but on the nature of their removal. In March 1966, 'I can see Clerys now the Pillar's gone' was sang with gusto.

Within his 1970 biography of Behan, Ulick O'Connor attributed the Gough poem to the writer, but later acknowledged Caprani's penmanship. It was an easy mistake to make, Caprani noting that 'no one came forward to claim authorship, and as Behan was one of the few people in Dublin in those days with both the courage and the cheek to use such four-letter words publicly', suspicion naturally fell on him. By the first payday after the Gough explosion, Caprani recounted that 'there were a couple of hundred nixered broadsheets of the ballad being passed from hand to hand in the boozing kens of the city centre.' It became an anonymous bestseller. More than a

---

11 Vincent Caprani, *Rowdy Rhymes and Rec-im-itations: Doggerel for a Departed Dublin* (Gill Books: Dublin, 1982).

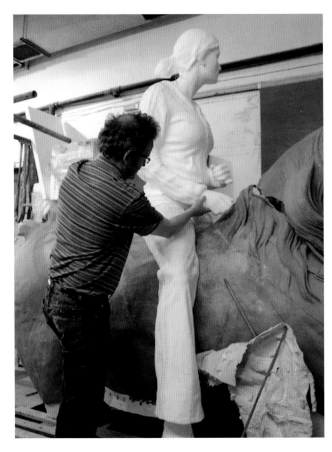

decade passed before Caprani admitted ownership of the poem to his father. Despite his objections to 'cornerboy language', he insisted it was 'better they blow up statues instead of people, wouldn't you say?'[12]

The afterlife of the Gough statue has been eventful. Sitting in storage at the Royal Hospital Kilmainham for many years, it was purchased by Robert Guinness in 1986 and now sits at Chillingham Castle in Northumberland, England. Guinness gifted the statue to Sir Humphrey Wakefield, a descendent of Gough. Reportedly, the statue was sold on the strict condition that it leave Ireland, such were

---

12 Ibid.

Garda fears of further attacks upon it. Within recently released State papers comes the observation that 'It is the garda view that nothing has happened in the meantime which would placate those who would wish to harm it. In their view, the climate is worse now than at the time of the last attack on the statue in 1957.'[13]

In 2010, the artist John Byrne completed a work which he called *Misneach*, taking its name from the Irish-language word for courage. Byrne's ambition was to create a sculpture that linked historic equestrian statues with the tradition of urban horse-riding in working-class Dublin. *Misneach* features a Ballymun local, teenager Toni Marie Shields, riding a steed cast from the statue of Gough's horse in Chillingham. Byrne approached Wakefield, recalling that 'I thought he would tell me to take a jump but he was delighted when I asked if I could copy his horse.'[14] A part of Gough's statue has returned to Dublin then, albeit with very different meaning. *Misneach* sits proudly outside the Ballymun Comprehensive School. Equestrian statues, once the preserve of the militarily and politically powerful, can take on new meaning in such circumstances.

Another little reminder of the Gough statue exists within the Phoenix Park, however, and James Flanagan was instrumental in its restoration. 'The statue was lit up in an unusual and unique way, as it had four special lamps. All of these lamps had reflectors set at an angle, and twenty-seven mirrors.' James remembers that the light was sent to William Sugg & Co. in England, a heritage lighting firm established in the 1830s. 'Instead of four mantles, there was six in each of the four lamps – to give the Gough statue extra light.' This lamp, which went on to be displayed in the Phoenix Park Visitor Centre, is the only surviving physical link to the Gough statue. 'We were approached about it by Dr John McCullen, who was the chief park superintendent at the time,' James remembers.

---

13 *The Irish Times*, 29 December 2019.   14 *The Irish Times*, 10 September 2010.

(left) The empty plinth of the Earl of Carlisle (Luke Fallon). (right) A view of the Earl of Carlisle monument from the Robert French Collection (Courtesy of National Library of Ireland).

Gough wasn't the only imperial monument lost in the Phoenix Park. The 7th Earl of Carlisle, another work by Foley which stood in the People's Gardens, was bombed a year later in 1958 by republicans. The plinth remains in the park today, complete with plaque. It recalls Daniel O'Connell's empty plinth outside City Hall, which now provides a home to a work by artist Alan Phelan. Who knows if something new will ever call the Earl of Carlisle's plinth home?

One imperial monument which isn't going anywhere is the Wellington Testimonial, a defining feature of the park and clearly visible from different parts of the city. Why Wellington Testimonial and not Wellington Monument? Arthur Wellesley, 1st Duke of Wellington, was still very much alive when the process of erecting the obelisk began. It was therefore not a form of memorialisation, but a statement of admiration. Neither name meant much to the Flanagans or other local children; it was simply the 'Mollymount'.

The Wellington Testimonial (Luke Fallon).

Despite its foundation stone being laid in 1817, the work remained unfinished until 1861, and in a lesser form than originally intended – gone was a planned statue of the duke on horseback. Still the largest obelisk of its kind in Europe, it stands at over sixty-two metres.

The Wellington obelisk has an interesting connection to the Flanagan family tree, albeit on the other side of the family. Frank recalls their grandfather, Lane, who also worked in the park but in a

This Eason collection images shows both the Wellington Testimonial and the Gough statue, helping to position the lost monument in the park (Courtesy of National Library of Ireland).

different capacity to Nicholas Flanagan, and who enjoyed a view most Dubliners could only dream of from the top of the obelisk:

> Around 1910, around that time, lightning struck the Wellington, and the top stone was dislodged. I don't know whether it came down or was just loosened. He was working in the depot as a handyman, and he was designated to help the steeplejack repair the Wellington. So the steeplejack put up the ladders, all the way up, and our grandfather went up the ladders. So he was at the top of the Wellington anyhow, helping the steeplejack. They had to put a lightning conductor on it.

Wellington is perhaps best remembered in his native city for words he never said, that 'being born in a stable does not make one a horse'.[15]

---

15 Rory Muir, *Wellington, Waterloo and the Fortunes of Peace 1814–1852* (London, 2015), 532.

THE WELLINGTON TESTIMONIAL, PHŒNIX PARK.

RESPECTFULLY DEDICATED TO THE COMMISSIONERS OF THE WELLINGTON TESTIMONIAL.

Fisher, Son & Cº London, 1829.

A fanciful view of the Wellington Testimonial, showing an intended (but never completed) statue of the Iron Duke alongside the obelisk (Courtesy of National Library of Ireland).

Instead, the words appear to come from Daniel O'Connell, mocking Wellington's perceived lack of Irishness. Wellington's real-life actions are commemorated in a series of bas-reliefs around the testimonial, made from melted French cannon, captured at Waterloo. The work of leading artists Joseph Robinson Kirk, Thomas Farrell and John Hogan, they know the military and political achievements of the 'Iron Duke'. An inscription tells us:

> *Asia and Europe, saved by thee, proclaim*
> *Invincible in war thy deathless name,*
> *Now round thy brow the civic oak we twine*
> *That every earthly glory may be thine.*

In Dublin, the Wellington Testimonial became 'the overgrown milestone', but its presence on the Northside wasn't an inevitability. Merrion Square and St Stephen's Green had both been explored as potential sites, but the residents of those fashionable quarters opposed the plans. At St Stephen's Green, the locals insisted that the already present statue of King George II must not give way to Wellington, the logic being that a sovereign could not be replaced by a mere subject. George II, like so many other equestrian statues in Dublin, fell to the dynamiters in May 1937, leaving no trace today.

During their own time working on Chesterfield Avenue, Frank and James became aware of a small act of commemoration, and a little cross in the grass which marks the site of the Phoenix Park assassinations of 1882, an event which shook Anglo-Irish relations and which occurred in broad daylight.[16]

Easy to miss, and almost directly across from the opening in the hedges that provides a stroller with a view into the grounds of the Áras, it is a curious thing that is open to very different interpretations.

---

16 Quoted in Pakenham, *Dublin: A Traveller's Companion*, 111.

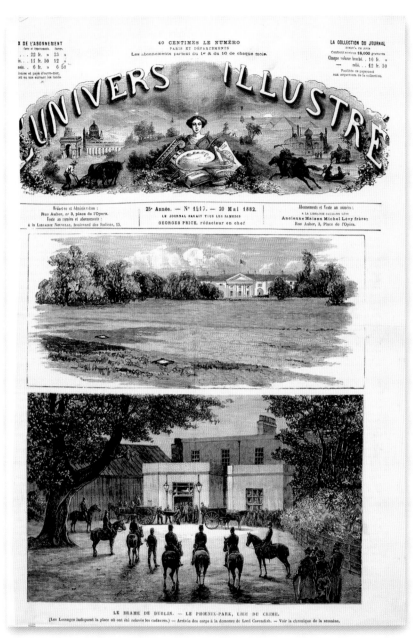

'Le Drame de Dublin. Le Phoenix-Park, lieu duy crime' – International coverage of the Phoenix Park Assassinations (Courtesy of National Library of Ireland).

Is it a monument to Burke and Cavendish, the men slain, or does it instead commemorate those who carried out the deed? Thomas Henry Burke, the Irish-born permanent under-secretary, was a hate figure to radical nationalists, denounced as the 'Castle Rat'. In private, Burke favoured Home Rule for Ireland and significant reforms, but that counted for little against his efficiency in the existing order. As Senan Molony, a historian of the park assassinations tells it, 'Unlike the transient placement of various administrations, Burke was the ever-present. His thirteen years of experience in a vital post had been relied on by many a grateful viceroy and chief secretary.'[17] By comparison, Cavendish had little to his name, on the first day of his post. Burke was most certainly the intended target, and Cavendish found himself in the wrong place at the wrong time.

The fear of the Fenians in the park was real, even before the killings. Of his own childhood, Churchill remembered how:

> My nurse, Mrs Everest, was nervous about the Fenians. I gathered these were wicked people and there was no end to what they would do if they had their way. On one occasion when I was out riding on my donkey, we thought we saw a long dark procession of Fenians approaching. I am sure now it must have been the Rifle Brigade out for a route march. But we were all much alarmed, particularly the donkey, who expressed his anxiety by kicking. I was thrown off and had concussion of the brain. This was my first introduction to Irish politics![18]

Known as the Invincibles, the men who struck on Chesterfield Avenue were members of a secret society *within* a secret society. An assassination team within the Fenian movement, the Invincibles

---

17 Senan Molony, *The Phoenix Park Murders: Conspiracy, Betrayal and Retribution* (Cork, 2006), 16. **18** Paul Bew, *Churchill and Ireland* (Oxford, 2016), 19.

The discovery of the corpses of Lord Frederick Cavendish and Thomas Henry Burke, as depicted in the contemporary press (Alamy).

emerged against the backdrop of tightening coercion laws and bitter suppression of the Land League movement. To their mind, 'there was no alternative but to meet the assassin rule of Britain by force'.[19] The Invincibles used surgical knives in targeting the men, and a contemporary newspaper report captured something that is still true about Chesterfield Avenue:

> The place where the tragedy occurred was an open highway. It is the leading road to the Viceregal Lodge, the Chief Secretary's residence and the residence of the Undersecretary and continues outwards to the country generally. In summer, it is an extremely popular walk, and at the time this crime was

19 Shane Kenna, *The Phoenix Park Assassinations and the Conspiracy that Shook an Empire* (Dublin, 2019), 50.

perpetuated there must have been hundreds of people within a short distance of the spot. Possibly, this was the reason the knife or dagger was resorted to instead of the revolver. The report of firearms would necessarily have attracted attention, and this from both quarters of the park, so that detection might easily have followed. This method adopted had the advantage of being silent and sure, no matter how savage; and as the result proved, the assassins got away without the faintest shadow.[20]

The dramatic story of the killings has been well told. Julie Kavanagh's *The Irish Assassins* paints a vivid picture, where the little details illuminate the tale. The Invincibles, waiting in the park, found themselves distracted by an ongoing game of polo. The poet Samuel Ferguson in his 1886 poem, 'At the Polo Ground', would give voice to their thoughts, as they waited to strike. Watching a game they regarded as imperial, but which still distracted them from the job at hand, as they wondered if their target would show:

> *Here I am*
> *Beside the hurdles fencing off the ground*
> *They've taken from us who have the right to it,*
> *For these select young gentry and their sport.*
> *Curse them! I would they all might break their necks!*
> *Young fops and lordlings of the garrison*
> *Kept up by England here to keep us down …*
> *And doubtless, as they dash along, regard*
> *Us who stand outside as a beggarly clue.*
> *'Tis half-past six. Not yet, no that's not her.*
> *Well, but 'tis pretty, sure, to see them stoop*
> *And take the ball, full gallop …*[21]

---

20 *The Northern Echo*, 8 May 1882, quoted in Ibid.   21 Julie Kavanagh, *The Irish Assassins: Conspiracy, Revenge and the Murders that Stunned an Empire* (London, 2022), 150.

SUPPLEMENT GIVEN AWAY WITH THE WEEKLY FREEMAN OF MAY 13th 1882 PRICE THREE HALF-PENCE

"WHAT VILLAINS HAVE DONE THIS?"

ERIN—" Before Heaven and men I repudiate and condemn this abominable act! They are my enemies who have perpetrated it."

'What villains have done this?' – a cartoon denouncing the killings from the *Weekly Freeman* (Courtesy of National Library of Ireland).

In the Flanagan family, this event was not some distant tale of assassination,but something which had occurred in a park their relatives were working in. As Frank recounted to me:

> My grandmother was in the Under-Secretary's Lodge, and she was present when that happened. She remembered all the to

and fro, the horses galloping crazily. She remembered being in the lodge, and the horses galloping up and down, which was very unusual in itself. Normally they'd be just trotting. But she remembered the police arriving, and the panic.

A general sense of confusion befell the park. 'The viceroy saw it from his window,' Frank tells me, 'but he thought it was just a fight between drunkards.' The Phoenix Park killings sent shockwaves through not just the British political establishment but also Irish nationalism. To Frank's mind, we must 'remember it was such a big thing politically, as well as everything else. It upended what Parnell was doing politically.' Charles Stewart Parnell, the 'uncrowned king of Ireland' in the eyes of the populace and a public figurehead of the Land League movement, lent his name to a manifesto in the immediate aftermath of the killings which condemned an act which had 'stained the name of hospitable Ireland'. Parnell would later be brought down by the scandal, ludicrous by contemporary standards, of his prior-mentioned love affair with Katharine O'Shea, the estranged wife of a Home Rule MP. Rather than 'Kitty O'Shea', a pejorative nickname bestowed on her, it could have been the words 'Phoenix Park' that became synonymous with his political downfall. He successfully weathered the storm that followed the 1882 killings.

Still, as historian Shane Kenna notes, there were others who felt very differently within Irish nationalism. A statement issued by the Executive of the Irish Republican Brotherhood shed no tears for 'the monster Burke, he has prayed upon the lives and liberties of his own countrymen for many years, and has deserved death a thousand times at our hands'.[22]

(opposite page) In the aftermath of the Phoenix Park assassinations and subsequent trials, postcard images of the victims and the Invincibles sold well across the city. This unusual item was a popular map, sold for one penny, depicting the Invincibles getaway (Courtesy of Dublin City Library and Archive).

---

22 Ibid., 98.

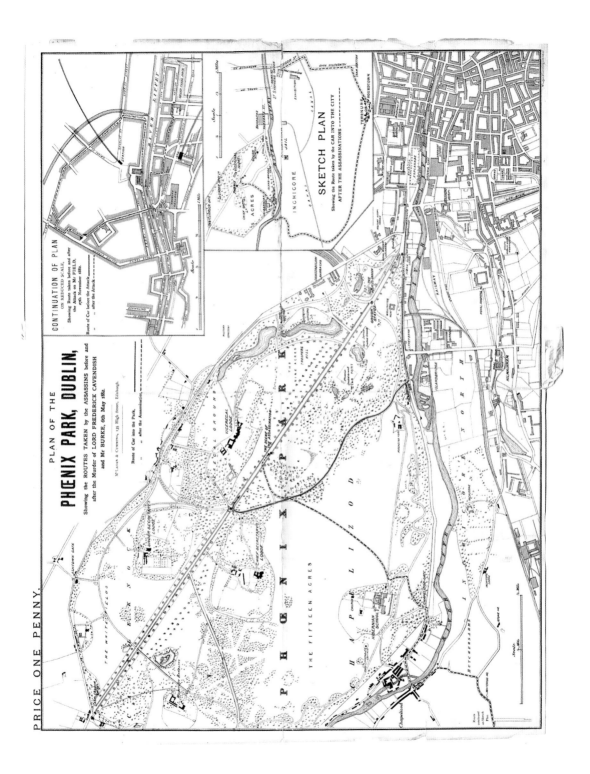

THE IRISH FRANKENSTEIN.

"The baneful and blood-stained Monster * * * yet was it not my Master to the very extent that it was my Creature ? * * * Had I not breathed into it my own spirit ?" * * * (*Extract from the Works of* C. S. P-RN-LL, M.P.

A contemporary *Punch* cartoon critical of Parnell and his relationship with the Fenians, depicting a movement he could not control (British Library).

Thomas Caffrey, Dan Curley, Joe Brady, Michael Fagan and Tim Kelly were hanged at Kilmainham Gaol for their involvement in the assassinations. James Carey, a leader of the conspiracy who had turned informer, had betrayed them. Carey was later assassinated by Patrick O'Donnell, a bricklayer, who learned of Carey's true identity as the informer set sail for Cape Town under a false name in the hope of escaping his past. In Dublin, *The New York Times* told readers there were celebrations on the news of Carey's demise: 'Eight enormous bonfires were built around Carey's late residence. There were also fires in other streets throughout the city. Bands marched through the streets playing national airs, followed by crowds of people, who cheered as they marched.'[23] O'Donnell's retribution on Carey even gets mention in George Desmond Hodnett's satirical 'Take Her Up to Monto', a song with several references to the Phoenix Park:

> *It wasn't very sensible*
> *To tell on the Invincibles*
> *They stand up for their principles, day and night.*

James Carey, the hunter who became the hunted, lost his place in the Irish nationalist pantheon by informing on his co-conspirators. Instead, his likeness ended up in Madame Tussaud's Chamber of Horrors, alongside replicas of the knives used. Also on display was a jaunting car used by the men in their getaway. Carey's name passed down the generations, synonymous with the risk of informing. The Invincibles are today buried in Kilmainham Gaol, with an ongoing campaign to have their bodies removed to Glasnevin Cemetery. If they ever make it there, they'll rest in the same graveyard as Thomas Henry Burke.

The events on Chesterfield Avenue, and the executions that followed, would long hold the imagination of Dubliners. James Joyce, the son of a faithful Parnellite, was obsessed by the killings and the

---

23 *The New York Times*, 2 August 1882.

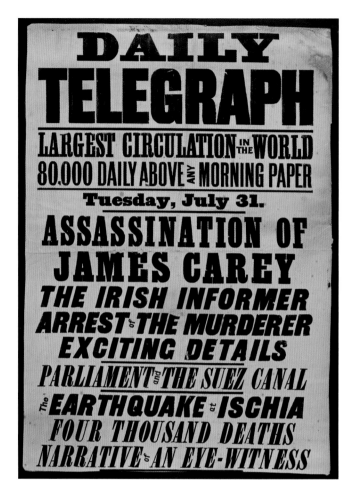

The death of James Carey was international news. He became 'the Irish informer' (Courtesy of National Library of Ireland).

manner in which they transformed the meaning of the Phoenix Park. The park emerges within *Dubliners* and *Ulysses*, and in the dream-like structure of *Finnegans Wake*. There, we find mention of 'the fenian's bark' and even more direct reference to the killings: 'our family furbear, our tribal tarnpike; quary was he invincibled and cur was he burked'.[24] Peculiarly, one of the most recalled names from the event

---

24 Lorraine Weir, 'Phoenix Park in *Finnegans Wake*', *Irish University Review* (Volume 5, Number 2, Autumn 1975), 230–49.

is that of James Fitzharris, a cab driver who assisted in the getaway. Frank remembers how 'he was known as Skin-the-Goat'. How he acquired such a colourful nickname remains the stuff of Dublin lore and debate, but there is little debate about the severity of the sentence handed down to him, serving sixteen years. One later Fenian recounted how the years took their toll:

> Years later when Mullett and Fitzharris, who was known as 'Skin-the-Goat', were released from Maryboro Prison, they arrived at Inchicore railway station on their way into town. They had just left the station when they saw a huge vehicle coming towards them. They became very frightened and thought the end of the world had come. The vehicle was actually an electric tram which they had not seen before.[25]

'It was never really forgotten,' Frank told me. 'I heard stories of it when young, and learned more and more of it with time. You'd sometimes see people at the little cross.' Frank is adamant too that others spoke of seeing ghostly figures in the park, connected with the event. 'One man would swear on seeing the figure of Burke, walking up the road alone.'

While it remains unclear just when or how the cross at the site was fixed into the grass along Chesterfield Avenue, there has been some kind of marker at the site since the late nineteenth century. On the first anniversary of the killings, one newspaper reported:

> Although the day was fine there were comparatively fewer people than usual in the Park, but still the fatal spot opposite the Viceregal Lodge was visited by a number of persons. Two crosses of ivy leaves, with wallflowers upon them,

---

25 Taken from Witness Statement WS1026, by James Clarke, part of the Bureau of Military History collection, courtesy of the Military Archives, Ireland.

denoted the places on the slope and the footpath where Lord Frederick Cavendish and Mr. Burke fell. These simple mementos, placed there by unknown hands, were the objects of sympathetic contemplation.[26]

The current commemorative cross has presumably been there for decades, and we can find reference to it in the accounts of some visitors to Dublin. James T. Farrell, the American novelist, visited the city in the 1940s and enjoyed the company of trade unionist Jim Larkin:

> He offered to take me around and show me various features of Dublin. We left his office, and entered his car. He asked me if I wanted to see the monument to the Invincibles. Jim's chauffeur drove us out to Phoenix Park. I imagined that I was going to see a statue, but this did seem passingly curious. The idea that there would be a monument commemorating the Invincibles in Dublin didn't make sense ...
> ... We got out. Jim walked along a path, looking down at the grass. I was bewildered. Jim became nervous, and he stared on the ground with some concern. Then he pointed. There it was. I saw a little hole where grass had been torn up. A cross had been scratched in the earth with a stick. I gathered that many Dubliners did not know of this act commemorating the Invincibles. Jim's boys always went out to Phoenix Park, and marked this cross in the earth. No matter how often grass was planted over it, it was torn up. The cross was marked in the earth.[27]

To Larkin, it was clearly a cross to the Invincibles themselves, and not their victims. Others viewed things very differently, and would leave

---

26 *Kerry Weekly News*, 12 May 1883. **27** James T. Farrell, 'Jim Larkin: Lest We Forget', *New International*, March 1947.

flowers to Burke and Cavendish on the anniversary of their deaths. For others still, it is not a question of allegiance but more the marking of a curious moment in the history of the park. For the folk singer and collector Frank Harte, the anniversary was a day to visit the memorial and sing a song related to the events. His friend Jerry O'Reilly of An Góilín, a Dublin singer's club, continues that tradition. There are any number of songs which are connected to the event, some condemning the killings and others celebrating them. There is even an array of songs dealing with the death of Carey, the informer. In one, Skin-the-Goat curses his old friend and longs for his demise:

> *When the equator is crossed may the rudder be lost*
> *And his vessel be wafted ashore*
> *To some cannibal isle near the banks of the Nile*
> *Where savages jump and roar*
> *With a big sharp knife may they take his life*
> *While his vessel is still afloat*
> *And pick his bones as clean as clean as stones*
> *Is the prayer of old Skin the Goat.*

Frank McNally, author of the 'An Irishman's Diary' column in *The Irish Times*, has written about how, when out running, he came upon a group of people gathered at the spot: 'I would have passed them without a thought except I happened to know they were standing at what must be Dublin's least visible historical monument.'[28] There is little about Dublin that is new to McNally, but the cross is news even to some who have walked or jogged by it a thousand times.

Still, confusion is introduced by the account of broadcaster and writer Matthew Byrne, whose 1987 *Dublin and Her People* speaks of the cross in the past tense, noting how 'for long enough, a cross set in

---

28 *The Irish Times*, 7 May 2019.

Lawrence Campbell's monument to Seán Heuston (Luke Fallon).

the road marked the assassination spot. It's gone now, and a jogger could pass the place nowadays, unaware of his brush with history.' To Byrne, the only lingering memorial to the events was in the lingo of the city, insisting that 'the whole sad episode gave Dubliners a new word. "Carey" is used to describe anyone who breaks faith and informs on his companions.'[29] So, has it come and gone over time?

Since independence, the commemorative landscape of the Phoenix Park has changed a bit. Now, we have Lawrence Campbell's figurative stone statue of executed 1916 leader Seán Heuston, unveiled not far from Carlisle's empty plinth in the People's Gardens. Unlike other imperial monuments in the park, there was never much fuss made about Wellington, a journalist noting in recent years that 'although this granite obelisk is, at 205ft tall, the largest in Europe, it excites little comment or controversy'.[30] The return of Gough or

---

29 Matthew Byrne, *Dublin and Her People* (Dublin, 1987), 9.   30 *Irish Independent*, 26 August 2003.

Carlisle seems unlikely, but so too does the removal of the Iron Duke. When asked what would happen if Gough returned to the Phoenix Park, Flank Flanagan laughed. 'Sure, you'd wonder if it would go up again!'

The idea of a specific place for displaying such monuments, like Budapest's Memento Park which houses many toppled Soviet memorials, appeals to me. *The Economist*, writing about a similar park in Lithuania, noted that 'As countries grapple with their unsavoury pasts and consider the rightful place of their controversial monuments, the park offers an alternative model to museums or destruction.'[31]

Whatever of Gough or Carlisle's own careers, the hand of John Henry Foley is one that Dublin can be proud of.

---

31 *The Economist*, 30 August 2017.

Frank and James Flanagan within their workshop (Luke Fallon).

CHAPTER SIX

Brothers on the Lights

For James Flanagan, understanding how things work is central to everything. In a small work shed, he demonstrated to me not only how the timers of gas lamps operate, but how they have evolved with time. 'I'll show you the mantles too, it's almost impossible to believe just how small and delicate they are.' Traditionally made of cotton, ramie or artificial silk, the tiny fabric bags generate a bright white light when heated by a flame. They're efficient, and they're incredibly delicate. 'We could go through 1,400 of them in a year.' While Frank Flanagan

A Map of the Phoenix Park within their workshop. It denotes every gas lamp in the space (Luke Fallon).

is clearly drawn to the history and heritage of the Phoenix Park gas lamps, James is always thinking of the future. 'Nearly everything we use now comes in from suppliers in Germany, and there are less and less companies working on these kind of lamps with the passing of time. I've often gone over to see what they're doing, and what they're developing. They're amazed that we're still at it in the Phoenix Park.' From very early on, James was interested in the *how* of the gas lamps, and seemingly everything else:

> Generally, I've always been very good with my hands. From the very start, I've been like that. You could say I was a meddler! I took a nice watch they had at home, a pocket

watch, and I took it apart. They were gone out somewhere at the time. I'd had my eye on the watch, it wasn't working well, and when they were out I took it apart. I wanted to know – how does this actually work? I still have that watch. But I'm still the same about everything, when I see something, I like to know how it actually works.

It wasn't an inevitability that Frank and James Flanagan would follow their grandfather and father into the family business. Frank recalls briefly joining An Garda Síochána as a young man in the 1950s, his eyes lighting up when I mentioned the famed Dublin policeman James Branigan, still remembered in the city as 'Lugs'. 'You'd see him on occasion down the courts, full of advice for younger fellas.' With the retirement of Tom Flanagan in the mid-1970s, the future of the gas lamps seemed to be in question, and it wasn't long before the Flanagan siblings found themselves exploring the idea of continuing the family tradition. The lamps themselves entered a strange period, suffering from a lack of maintenance, Frank recalling:

> When they weren't wound, they weren't working. Any lights that were on seemed to stay on. That baked the carbon into the glass, a very difficult thing to clean and remove. They were lighting more or less continuously for nine months, and someone in the Dáil even raised the gas lamps in the Phoenix Park.

Other issues around the Phoenix Park were being raised in the Dáil too, including the increase in traffic as suburbanisation continued apace in Dublin. Eileen Lemass, who represented the fast-growing Dublin West, even raised the idea of a new ring road:

> I see that the Minister is seeking ways and means of improving the traffic through the Phoenix Park which has become a

great problem in recent years. There are new housing estates at Chapelizod, Castleknock and so on, which have increased the traffic through the Phoenix Park considerably in the last few years. This is a great pity. It is probably not practicable or possible but I should like to see most of that traffic routed through some other area. Possibly a new ring road could be built that would syphon off a lot of the very heavy traffic at present using the Phoenix Park. Is it a park or a highway? It is becoming a highway.[1]

Other things seemed destined to become highways too. Who today could believe that some seriously pondered the idea of concreting Dublin's canals, as a solution to the traffic gridlock, or that there would be a car for every five people living in the greater Dublin metropolitan area, unimaginable just a decade or two ago? One influential Phoenix Park resident, the wife of the American Ambassador, described the busy nature of the park in her memoir of living there, as 'new suburban housing estates springing up on the far side are bringing thousands of commuters into Dublin through the park.' It wasn't all traffic jams, but also speeding cars which alarmed her, recalling that 'the speed and carelessness with which they make their morning and evening circuit on the main road are frightening, and the plethora of accidents is tragic.'[2]

With all of this increased traffic came debates about the Phoenix Park and its core function. Was it to be a place of recreation, or a busy place that connected city and suburbia? Within the discussion, some called for modernisation of the lighting of Chesterfield Avenue. In the words of one TD, 'The Park has quaint nineteenth-century gas lighting and, while it looks well, it is not effective.'[3]

---

1 Dáil Éireann debate, 13 April 1978 (Houses of the Oireachtas. Volume 305, Number 5). 2 Elizabeth Shannon, *Up in the Park: The Diary of the Wife of the American Ambassador to Ireland* (New York, 1983), 213. 3 *Evening Herald*, 30 May 1979.

The 1970s was a curious time for the Phoenix Park. In newspapers and the Dáil, there was talk of traffic, and concern for the park's perceived decline. Yet it also hosted one of the defining moments of the Irish twentieth century, with the visit of Pope John Paul II in September 1979. The journalist Nell McCafferty captured the mood of the million-plus crowd: 'The ushers and orderlies and security men were redundant. A joyfully corralled nation behaved as if blessed, and thought itself blessed, and was blessed when he stood atop his Popemobile and was driven up and down and through our serried ranks, so that no one was far from him, and the Irish people felt as close to God as it was possible to be.'[4] It is often an outsider who most clearly sees the significance of an event. Elizabeth Shannon, wife of the American ambassador, captured the contrast of the day with earlier times of repression. To her mind, 'it was a long, hard road from a tiny mass rock in the wilds of Mayo or the mountains of Kerry, to the tall white cross in the middle of the Phoenix Park.' While older generations of Irish people had experienced such repression, she felt that 'they can tell them another, happier story now, of how they were brought as babes to the Phoenix Park and held up high over their da's head to receive the papal blessing.'[5]

Both Frank and James have strong recollections of the visit. For Frank, it seemed to transport Blackhorse Avenue back to an earlier time:

> First of all, I remember the build-up to it. The streamers and flags on every road around here, it must have been like the Eucharistic Congress. A day or two before it, all traffic was stopped on these roads. People were out, literally walking on the road, like in a time before so many cars. On the day of the

---

4 Mary Kenny (ed.), *3 Days in September: When the Pope Came to Ireland* (Dublin, 2004), 118. 5 Shannon, *Up in the Park*, 207.

arrival of the pope, houses that were nearest to the park like ours were out at three o'clock in the morning, and processed through the Ashtown Gate. Ballyfermot, Chapelizod and the like came in from the other end of it. Others from Parkgate Street. It was people marching from the early morning until about eleven o'clock.

Even in the built landscape, you can still see traces of the papal visit. Most obviously, there is the impressive cross in the park, located in its centre, the work of Scott Tallon Walker Architects. Ronnie Tallon remembered a phone call from the archbishop of Dublin just eight weeks out from the visit: 'We decided that we required a cross the height of Nelson's Pillar, which was 125 feet high, which would be clearly visible to all from the furthest reaches of the vast congregation and which would give a sense of focus to the occasion.'[6] It came into the park in sections, and was welded into its final form on the ground. They lifted it into place on 14 September 1979, which happened to be the date of the church's Feast of the Exaltation of the Cross.[7] James Flanagan remembers how 'I was there on the arrival of that. And to me, on the ground, it looked absolutely massive. I can remember the crane, that lifted it in one piece. I don't think anyone imagined at first it would be a permanent thing, but I remember being amazed by it on seeing it go up.' In addition, there are other, more subtle things around the Phoenix Park that also recall the visit, as James pointed out on Blackhorse Avenue: 'You might notice, opposite Cumiskey's pub there, the wall was literally knocked down all the way along to make way for the flow of people coming out. You can still see the newer part of the wall, near the turnstile.'

In the great mass of people, Frank and James both recall the moment the pope first flew over the crowd. For Frank:

---

6 Ibid., 215. 7 Ibid., 216.

The impressive 1979 Papal Cross. Intended to 'give a sense of focus to the occasion' (Luke Fallon).

We got in only about a hundred metres from the pope's cross. Then, the word came that the pope's plane was on its way. It was like a 747, it came up the Chesterfield Avenue way, so to speak, and then veered left over the Fifteen Acres. As the plane came over the Fifteen Acres, it dipped to the right, you could see the pope in the windows of the thing, and he waving out. That was the moment, everyone said it was like an apparition. Whatever about seeing it on television, it just couldn't be the same as seeing that there.

James recalls not only that sight, but the sound: 'When the plane came over, the one thing I remember was the roar of the crowd. That was massive. You can imagine a million and a quarter people roaring at the same time, amidst the waving of flags. I don't think I'll ever forget that, or that anyone else there could either!' While the day brought back memories of the 1932 Eucharistic Congress, the bigger question facing the Phoenix Park was the future.

Then came the appointment of John McCullen as chief superintendent in August 1984. Talking to both Frank and James, it's almost as if the Phoenix Park they know can be divided into two eras: 'before' and 'after' McCullen. In Frank's view, McCullen deserves enormous credit for promoting the heritage of the Phoenix Park:

> Dr John McCullen was very conscious of what was around him, and he really wished to not only save things as they were but to protect them going forward. He retained what was original, he repaired what was damaged, and what was lost – in so far as was possible – was thankfully restored. Things like the colours of lamp standards, or how the park would have looked in the Victorian times, he thought a lot about all of these things.

McCullen's appointment attracted significant press attention, as he emphasised the need to be ambitious in thinking about the park and its possibilities. In March 1985, he launched a major tree-planting programme, designed to counter the negative impact of Dutch elm disease which had greatly reduced the park's tree numbers. According to McCullen, it was 'the first step in a plan to bring the famous Dublin recreational area back to its former glory'.[8] For the new chief

---

8 *Evening Herald*, 22 March 1985.

superintendent, the past and future of the park were undeniably linked. A journalist wrote of how, 'to charges that changing the look of the Phoenix Park is like spray-painting the Mona Lisa and is bound to upset conservatives, John McCullen responds that in almost every respect he is being faithful to the Phoenix Park of old'.[9] There was also hope that other issues too could be addressed, with the press reporting on how 'a major clampdown on traffic using the Phoenix Park and its restoration as a national historic park are now top priorities'.[10] The gas lamps featured in this vision too:

> On Phoenix Park's fittings, the Superintendent says that the famous gas lamps that adorn the Park will be restored. 'In a lot of cases, the lamps themselves have gone missing. We are now discussing with Dublin Gas and the Department of Energy the possibility of replacing these lamps in the same triple mantle design.' The Phoenix Park visitor today would also notice that the lamps are being repainted. 'The original deep green colour didn't particularly highlight the beauty of the lamp in the green environment of the Park.'[11]

Frank recalls the very beginning of this new era in the Phoenix Park: 'I can remember going to meet McCullen with my father. He talked of how fantastic it would be if we could stay involved. At the time, we'd a few more involved in it, and we mostly did shift work. It was something we could all give a bit of time to.' When I asked Frank and James if they felt any push from their father to follow on from him and continue a legacy, they both instead point to the deep affection McCullen clearly had for the park as something that opened them up to the possibility.

One broadcaster who took a keen interest in the work McCullen was doing was Joe Duffy, recalling making a radio documentary about the Phoenix Park as a young would-be broadcaster in a competition

---

9 *Evening Press*, 26 July 1985. 10 *Evening Press*, 13 November 1985. 11 *Evening Press*, 26 July 1985.

(left and below)
The unveiling of the newly
restored Phoenix Park
gas lamps (with thanks to
John McCullen).

THE LAMPLIGHTERS OF THE PHOENIX PARK

for the chance to work in RTÉ. 'I hit upon the idea of a journey in a horse and carriage through the park. But of course, I had not yet learned the first rule of radio: keep it simple.' Duffy's broadcast was not without its challenges, and 'as the horse box arrived early one Sunday morning and the handlers battled to harness the giddy horses to the very fragile carriage, I wondered why I simply hadn't got the sound effects from the vast RTÉ library!' Duffy's interview with the 'extraordinarily knowledgeable park superintendent John McCullen and the gifted arboriculturist Noel O'Shea' marked the beginning of a broadcasting career.[12]

For the sum of £150,000, the Phoenix Park gas lamps were restored, and unveiled in April 1988. The timing was perfect, with the city deep in nostalgia during the celebrations for Dublin's so-called 'Millennium'. While historians were quick to point out that the city's foundation owed more to 841 than 988, 1988 is still a year many recall fondly. As historian Rebecca Boyd describes it:

> In 1986, the Corporation decided that a millennium celebration was needed to boost the city's morale, deep in economic recession. This marked a step forward for the city, and a step away from the Wood Quay debacle, and made Dublin the first town in Ireland to celebrate its Viking heritage. In a year-long celebration of the city, the Corporation went to great lengths to encourage civic pride. They released special edition 1988 Dublin milk bottles, planted 1,000 trees and 500,000 flowering plants, floated a statue of Gulliver (from Swift's *Gulliver's Travels*) down the Liffey, unveiled public sculptures, planned a new Viking Adventure Centre, and issued a 1988 Millennium fifty pence piece. Whilst historians criticised the accuracy of the chosen date, the public thoroughly enjoyed

---

12 Joe Duffy, *Just Joe: My Autobiography* (Dublin, 2011). Duffy's *Liveline* programme on RTÉ Radio 1 has featured several episodes on the Phoenix Park.

James Flanagan demonstrating how the timers of the lamps work (Luke Fallon).

these celebrations, and even now children of the 1980s reminisce about the millennium milk bottles.[13]

There were now four mantles in each lamp instead of two, in an attempt to bring more light. 'There were also more lights than before,' Frank points out. 'Lamp standards were cast by Leinster Foundry in Athy, and lanterns were fabricated by David Woods in Tallaght. The time switch system was extended from seven-day service to fourteen-day service. They still had to be inspected nightly.'

The lights that Frank and James care for are not just located on and around Chesterfield Avenue. They also clean lamps within the grounds

---

13 Rebecca Boyd, 'Raiding the Vikings: How Does Ireland Consume Its Viking Heritage?' in Tom Birkett and Roderick Dale (eds), *The Vikings Reimagined: Reception, Recovery, Engagement* (Michigan, 2019), 232–49, at 232.

A lamp standard fixed in place in the workshop for repair (Luke Fallon).

of Áras an Uachtaráin, an institution that has opened up considerably to the public in recent times with the civic parties and celebrations hosted by President Michael D. Higgins and his wife Sabina. James points out that 'the trees in there tell their own story. You have trees planted by visiting presidents, and trees planted by Queen Victoria. The entire history of the place is there in them.' Today, the most recognisable feature of the Áras grounds is perhaps the Peace Bell, symbolically positioned between two oak trunks – one from Dublin and one from Antrim. The base of the bell is of Glendalough quartz, which 'recalls an ancient, uncontested Boyne Valley site that has forever been part of the shared history of all Irish men and women'.[14] In earlier times, it was a lamplighter of a different kind who provided the Áras with its most recognisable symbol. President Mary Robinson, elected to the office in 1990, placed a symbolic lamp in the window of the house which would send a message to the diaspora and those who had left Ireland in search of new lives:

> The idea of the light in the window appealed to me. I had promised, in my acceptance speech, that 'there will always be a light on in Áras an Uachtaráin for our exiles and our emigrants'. For health and safety reasons, of course, we couldn't have a naked flame, so we had a lamp made in the shape of a candle – with no 'off' button – and put it on the window sill of our family kitchen upstairs, which was under the main portico of the house and could be seen from the public road. I hoped that emigrants would learn of the symbol and know that we at home in Ireland were thinking about them, felt connected to them and understood if they were lonely or in need of support.[15]

---

14 Elizabeth Mayes (ed.), *Áras an Uachtaráin: A History of the President's House* (Dublin, 2013), 46.
15 Mary Robinson, *Everybody Matters: A Memoir* (London, 2012), 157.

Frank and James Flanagan at the Áras gates (Luke Fallon).

(opposite and above) A historic lamp at the rear of the Áras, the last of its kind in use (Luke Fallon).

Asked if they have particularly fond memories of any former president, both instantly cite Mary McAleese. She was, as they recall, especially interested in the day-to-day running of the Phoenix Park beyond the gates of the Áras. While many dream of being invited into the home of a president, this president wished to visit everyone else. As James tells it:

> She was interested in the people, but also the heritage of the Phoenix Park. She visited all of the cottages across the park, each and every one of them at different times, and would have tea with them all. Every lodge house, every family who worked within the grounds had that happen. She was very neighbourly, and viewed the Áras as part of a community.

President McAleese not only ingrained herself into the community within the Phoenix Park, she also opened the Áras to visitors, recalling

Within the Flanagan workshop, where everything from a deer antler to mantles can be found (Luke Fallon).

how 'the Áras was to be a welcoming place, especially to those who had never considered visiting it. The first thing to do was to open the house to the general public.'[16]

At the rear of the Áras is a favourite lamp of Frank and James, owing to its prestige. James told me how 'the lamp on the wall there, going back to the days of the Royal Irish Constabulary station, is still on an original seven-day timer'. Operating on the same mechanics as the later timers, these had to be wound weekly instead of biweekly. They also care for lamps in the Grangegorman Military Cemetery, just across Blackhorse Avenue from the Áras. If Glasnevin has become Ireland's national cemetery, and a place of nationalist pilgrimage, this place is something else entirely, and a reminder of British Army (though often Irishmen) fatalities in the turbulent times that led to independence. How many of us have stepped into it, to see the headstones of Sherwood Foresters who lost their lives in the bloodbath on Mount Street Bridge during the Easter Rising, or the grave of Martin Doyle, who received the Victoria Cross for bravery during the First World War? In a colourful life, Doyle later joined the Irish Republican Army and fought in the War of Independence. It certainly makes him a unique story in this military cemetery.

There were some things about the Phoenix Park that recalled earlier decades, like the re-emergence of motor racing as a hugely popular sport in the 1970s and '80s. 'But now,' Frank joked, 'the cars were a bit faster.' In the same year that the new gas lamps were unveiled, the *Evening Herald* reported in 1988 on how 'for the last two weeks workmen have been transforming the Park into a proper racing circuit. Cats' eyes have been lifted, gas lamps have been protected, a spectator bridge has been built and five miles of barriers have been erected.'[17] Tens of thousands would observe the high-speed racing.

Working in the park has meant that the brothers are accustomed to seeing just about everything within it, and understanding that it

---

16 Mary McAleese, *Here's the Story: A Memoir (2020).* **17** *Evening Herald,* 12 August 1988.

can be a very different place in the dark hours. The park – like any sizeable park in an urban setting – has long had a reputation as a place which attracts some seeking sexual encounters. There is nothing new in any of this. The park gains mention as a 'cruising' location in the diaries of Roger Casement, describing an encounter there.[18] Not long after independence, one nationalist newspaper complained of how 'women of bad character are plying their terrible trade there with the utmost affrontery, and an open display of vice is carried on without any action against it being taken by the authorities'.[19] Frank noted that his father had encountered this dimension of the park:

> My father told me he was going through the park one night, it must have been in the thirties or forties. He said there was a horse and cab, down the road by the McKee Barracks, and that two detectives found four fellas in the cab, acting up. They were arrested – and they each got four years imprisonment.

Even in George Desmond Hodnett's 'Take Her Up to Monto', previously alluded to for its depiction of the aftermath of the 1882 assassinations, we find mention of this dimension of the Phoenix Park. 'Buckshot Forster', a nickname bestowed upon William Edward Forster who advocated lethal force against the Land League movement, is described as having 'took a mot and lost her up the Furry Glen'. While 'The Zoological Gardens', a humorous song from the Behan songbook, clearly has nothing whatsoever to do with the innocence of a day out in Dublin Zoo and more to do with other possibilities in the park:

> *We went out there on our honeymoon*
> *Says she to me 'If you don't come soon*

---

18 See Roger Sawyer, *Roger Casement's Diaries: 1910 – The Black and the White* (London, 1997). 19 *Honesty*, 10 July 1926.

I'll have to get in with the hairy baboons'
Up in the Zoological Gardens.
Says she to me 'It's seven o'clock
And it's time for me to be changin' me frock
For I love to see that old cockatoo'
Up in the Zoological Gardens.

This world was all just part and parcel of working the beat of the Phoenix Park. James jokes about it:

> When you'd see a guy walking up the park, with a Mac raincoat under his arm and a girl on the other side, you knew they were going up to lie in the grass! They'd lay that in the grass. You took note of where they were going, and when they were finished there were always coins or maybe a parker pen that fell out of his pocket! They were one group of fellas who didn't have any love for the lamplighters.

Motor racing and courting lovers then, in their own peculiar ways, each created their own tradition. One of the physical features of the park which appears historic is surprisingly new: the five gas lamps on the Mountjoy Cross roundabout. Near the Castleknock gate of the park, and named after nearby Mountjoy House which today houses the Ordnance Survey of Ireland, this 2009 addition is something that John McCullen insists 'the Flanagans were absolutely integral to'.

To James, 'that was a great job, to have five gas lamps beside each other. The belief was that if one came on, it would stop the others from doing the same, as they'd think it was daylight'. Frank recalled how 'the Germans who supply parts to us said it couldn't be done. Not only the lights from one light interfering, but that it would be interfered with by headlights from cars.' He had faith in his brother to devise a solution:

The light cell in the lamp was affected by the headlights of cars, so what we did was he made copper ferrules to go down over the lamp censors, so that the lamp was only taking in the light from the top, not from the sides. The daylight censors, he wired the lot of them together, and brought them up to the very top of the middle lamp ... So, we proved the Germans wrong! That was all the brainchild of Jimmy.

To be out working on the gas lamps of the Phoenix Park can involve unusual hours, and means that days off enjoyed by just about everyone else can be working days like any other. I was curious if this impacted on relationships. Frank married June O'Loughlin, a Tipperary woman, in the early 1960s. 'She was amenable for anything! Before I worked

The Mountjoy Cross roundabout (Luke Fallon).

Detail of the five lamps at the Mountjoy Cross (Luke Fallon).

in the park I was in a bookie's, but she didn't mind that and she didn't mind the lights.' James married Anne Lane, who 'encouraged me all the time into it'. It's one aspect of the job that thankfully has changed with the passing of time. Could Nicholas Flanagan have imagined the fourteen-day timer, when he and his brothers lit and extinguished every lamp individually?

Both Frank and James are still fascinated by the Phoenix Park, and conscious that it is made up of many different parts. Just as they are the descendants of one tradition, they speak of the deer as having a long claim to the place. 'For me, it's one of the sounds of the park. The crashing of the horns at certain times of year,' James says. Frank talks of how 'at night, they can move across the park,

James Flanagan attending to a gas lamp (Luke Fallon).

James Flanagan with a lamp standard in need of replair, demonstrating the size of the individual lamp (Luke Fallon).

over near to where I am'. The deer are one of the few things that have been around the Phoenix Park longer than the Flanagans. 'We still climb the same steps our forefathers did. We walk the path of the Invincibles, of Cavendish and Burke, of dukes, viceroys, kings and queens, of presidents and even Pope John Paul II.'

Paddy Hunter, Dublin
Corporation Lamplighter
(Courtesy of Dublin City
Library & Archive).

James and Frank Flanagan, April 2023 (Luke Fallon).

CHAPTER SEVEN

Keeping the Lights On: The Phoenix Park Today

Ireland is a great nation. And we are great people. We have experienced hardship and struggle before. We have overcome many trials in the past with our determination and our spirit. We will prevail.[1]

On 12 March 2020, less than a week before Ireland's national holiday, Leo Varadkar addressed the Irish public from Washington DC. The message was clear: we were

---

1 Speech of Leo Varadkar, 12 March 2020. https://merrionstreet.ie/en/news-room/news/statement_by_an_taoiseach_leo_varadkar_on_measures_to_tackle_covid-19_washington_12_march_2020.html.

The Parkgate Street entrance of the Phoenix Park (Luke Fallon).

entering into a period of tremendous challenge, but would overcome it.

Then, we knew little of just what exactly lay ahead. Televised images from Italian emergency wards, coupled with public outrage at the ongoing Cheltenham Festival, set the mood. How to behave and interact with one another remained unclear, but one thing was quickly apparent: it was better to be outside than indoors.

It said much about the fast-moving nature of the pandemic, and the absence of clarity around what was fine and what wasn't, that the

A gas lamp on North Road, its timer clearly visible (Luke Fallon).

taoiseach himself was soon in hot water for socialising with friends in the Phoenix Park. The *Irish Mirror* newspaper headline was not a statement but a question: 'Did Leo Varadkar break any rules while sunbathing in the Phoenix Park?'[2] In the end, the paper told us, he hadn't. The taoiseach 'was also in a group of four, which is allowed

---

2 *Irish Mirror*, 25 May 2020.

outdoors, and appeared to be keeping a distance between the two friends that he is not living with'.[3]

Even at the time of writing, in the first half of 2023, such things can feel like ancient history. Who amongst us did not sit in a park in the company of friends? Yet for those who work in the Phoenix Park, including the Flanagan family, it is a time that will never be forgotten. Staff of the park talk about the pandemic as one of the great historic challenges the place has faced – and one in which it played a central and positive part.

On a cold and wet morning in March 2023, I made my way up the North Road, turning at the Mountjoy Cross on Chesterfield Avenue. I wanted to meet some of the key figures in the administration of the park to discuss its contemporary existence, and the impacts of recent history. This area, for most visitors, is uncharted territory. The route brings you to an important centre of administration without which the park could not function, but which almost no visitors are aware of. Within what is called The Whitefields are offices, maintenance buildings, yards, storage sheds, communal and canteen facilities and everything else imaginable. The Phoenix Park functions because the people who work in The Whitefields turn up each day. The Whitefields is also home to the beautiful Park Superintendent's Lodge, constructed in a cottage orné style in the 1830s by Jacob Owen, architect to the Board of Works. Architecturally fine, it nonetheless had its issues, as John McCullen highlighted:

> The house, two and a quarter miles from the Dublin gate, had no road serving it for over a quarter of a mile, even though it was located in one of the swampiest areas of the park. The house required decoration and some alterations, to make it a comfortable residence; externally there was a need for sheds, a carpenter's yard, a covered sawpit and domestic offices.[4]

---

3 Ibid. 4 John McCullen, *An Illustrated History of the Phoenix Park: Landscape and Management to 1880* (Dublin, 2009), 259.

McCullen, foremost historian of the Phoenix Park and the former park superintendent who salvaged much more than the gas lamps, knows much about this house. He lives in it. And, in the broadest sense, he still lives the Phoenix Park.

The journey of understanding every aspect of the park's growth, development and climate will never end. On first meeting McCullen, I quickly learned the depth of his historic knowledge; for example, I wondered if many people were aware of the prior-mentioned cross marking the site of the Phoenix Park assassinations. 'There's huge interest in it,' he tells me. 'Queen Victoria wanted a monument on the spot.' Perhaps unsurprisingly – and maybe fortunately given the fate of some memorials in the park – it never came to be. Only McCullen could inform you of the surprising but fascinating little titbit that the date of Tony Blair and Bertie Ahern's 2003 meeting and press conference in the Phoenix Park's Farmleigh House was the same date, 6 May, as the killings. No journalist noted the significance of the date in Anglo-Irish history.

McCullen was inside the park throughout the recent pandemic; for the rest of us, of course, the great question was if we could be too.

Sitting across the table from me in The Whitefields, along with McCullen, were Margaret Gormley, chief park superintendent, and park superintendent Paul McDonnell. I began by asking about the challenges and opportunities of recent times. For Gormley, March 2020 heralded significant changes:

> We became an oasis for a new generation who had never visited parks before. Because of Covid, a lot of people who lived in apartments had no outdoor space. So, we had these new visitors, coming to the Phoenix Park for perhaps the first time, and we now had to ask – how can we accommodate them?

She jokes that she is 'a relatively short time here, at some twenty-plus years!' Still, no one in the park had to contend with a pandemic before, regardless of their tenure. There was a lot of quick thinking required, and the Phoenix Park had to work within the guidelines of the day, which could be ever-changing. Dublin felt claustrophobic, with two-kilometre restrictions in place, allowing citizens to wander just that distance from their own front door. In time, this broadened to five kilometres, and at that point the walls of the Phoenix Park were within travelling distance of people from communities as geographically diverse as Palmerstown, Cabra, Blanchardstown and the inner city. Paul McDonnell remembers how:

> We did a lot of research, and we looked up the five kilometres, how many people could possibly be in that five kilometres? We found over half a million people. While some were saying there were too many people in the park, they were all within their five kilometres.

For many of us, the Phoenix Park represented a great freedom in the loosening restrictions. Gormley insists that not alone did 'the public gain a new appreciation for parks', but the very meaning of the Phoenix Park seemed to evolve. With restrictions in place on traffic, it was 'no longer just a through-route for vehicles, and we were then able to come out and say that well, actually, that's not the number one priority. The park is for people.'

During the early days of McCullen's tenure, newspaper coverage of the Phoenix Park had obsessively focused on its traffic congestion. Now, the unimaginable happened. As Gormley tells it, 'We could never envision, in John's time or mine, that there would be no parking on Chesterfield Avenue.' The day we met, we realised, marked a significant milestone. 'It's exactly three years since a car parked on Chesterfield Avenue,' McDonnell informed us.

The Phoenix Park exists within a much broader network of parks in Dublin, and communication between parks was constant throughout the early stages of the pandemic. People were encouraged to maintain a distance of two metres from each other, but what did that actually look like? Beyond these issues of physical safety though, Gormley pointed out that there were other health challenges. People wanted to be outside, but what about those who felt particularly vulnerable, and maybe anxious of being in crowded places, outdoors or otherwise?

> The recreational spaces – the parks – were hugely important for mental and physical health. We all had to move quite quickly, to try and transform our spaces to deal with all these people ... Cocooning was a huge issue. How could you get the elderly into open space safely? We actually zoned the Visitor Centre walled garden as a cocooning space for older visitors.

Everyone then could have their own park within the park. McDonnell jokes of how 'there seemed to be new walking trails, people would walk off the paths in all directions, to be alone. You'd see the newly trod paths of walkers.' Still, people moving like deer across the unpaved terrain was a good thing. McDonnell asks a simple but pertinent question: 'Isn't this what parks are really about? It's not just about getting a car from A to B, it's about people enjoying themselves.'

Throughout the pandemic, or what seemed to become known in Dublin colloquial speak as 'the covid', the Phoenix Park was a transformed place. One of the few consistent features were the gas lamps. Just as before, they came on and off each day. For McCullen, who has examined the park from its pre-history to its contemporary existence, they represented a link with tradition in what was a rapidly changing situation. Of the Flanagans, he insists that 'they've so much invested, it's in their DNA'.

As the time switches and mechanisms in the gas lamps are nearly a hundred years old, their reliability is less than perfect. This requires nightly inspection and inspection some mornings. For a lamplighter, the day begins at sunset. This varies from 4.15 p.m. in midwinter to 10.15 p.m. in summer.

One sound we often hear at dusk is that of the barn owl from the woods on Chesterfield Avenue. Our work can require close inspection of each light, which sometimes show a lack of luminosity because of jet blockages.

Across the Fifteen Acres we can meet herds of deer. These have been in the west end of the Fifteen Acres during the day, and now move to fresh grazing in the east end, without interference from dogs or people. As we come near the Furry Glen we meet four or five foxes. At the Furry Glen itself we sometimes encounter badgers.

When a lamp light is brighter than normal it can indicate a fire in the mechanism; this can result from a leak in connections loosened by the vibrations of traffic.

Next morning, the same lamplighter checks his list of misfires, gets the appropriate tools together and sets out to rectify each lamp with a problem. This can take up to three or four hours depending on the cause of the problem. For three days in each fortnight, the full team gives each lamp its fourteen-day service. This includes winding the clocks in each lamp, as well as glass-cleaning, mantle-replacing, clearing carbon blockages caused by burning gas, lubricating moving parts and setting their light-up and light-off times. It is a pleasure working in the Phoenix Park, where we mix with all types of people and wildlife.

James Flanagan

That the lights stayed on was, in a small way, a symbolic act. The park had fallen into darkness in the days of the Emergency, but this too was a thing that would pass. For Gormley, the gas lamps are one of the features that give to the Phoenix Park its unique feeling and character:

> They set the context for the Phoenix Park, in a sense ... For visiting dignitaries of heads of State, it very much adds to the feeling of the Áras, coming up that road. We would liaise with colleagues abroad, and one of the key features that interests park people, say the royal parks in London, is that the Phoenix Park kept gas lights. That is so unique.

Under McCullen, the Phoenix Park produced its first Conservation Plan in 1986, which Gormley points out was 'the first conservation

The author interviewing Frank and James Flanagan in the Phoenix Park, April 2023 (Luke Fallon).

plan of its kind in Europe'. The more recent plan, published in 2011, reaffirms the commitment of the park to gas lamps. A low level of light pollution lends itself to everything from star-gazing to the wildlife of the park. To Gormley, 'it's hugely important for biodiversity ... This is actually a habitat. We've over eight hundred and fifty species in the Phoenix Park.'

The pandemic raised dilemmas for the Flanagan family. At eighty-nine when the country went into lockdown, Frank is part of a cohort that was encouraged to limit social interactions as much as possible. However, the family business in recent years has extended to sons-in-law and grandchildren:

> When we got on a bit, we recognised that we had to have a follow-up, and if we could get a follow-up in our own family, all the better! I had a son-in-law, and Jimmy had a son-in-law, and we recognised that they could manage to do the gas work as well as their own work.

Neither Ronan nor John are 'new' to the industry, with Ronan coming on board in 2008 and John in 2010. Both have personal connections to the Phoenix Park area, with Ronan previously based in McKee Barracks. For John, the park is an especially emotive place:

> I think we all have some connection with the park in this area. My father died in the park, he had gone out for a run, one Saturday morning in 1984, and he had a heart attack and died. He dropped dead at lamp number 54. I always used to think it was fate, that I would end up working in the park, and to be walking past where he died four or five times a week.

Ronan's son Connor has also worked on the gas lamps. There are reminders of how Frank and James talk of their own childhoods, in hearing Ronan describe how 'Jimmy would bring him to the shed, and

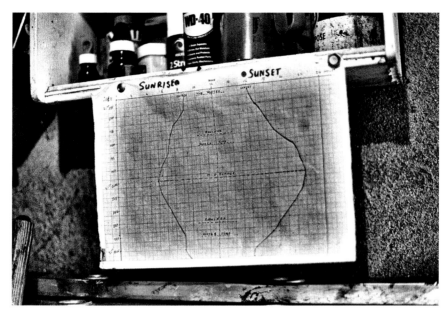

Sunrise and sunset, a simple but important document which informs the work of the lamplighters (Luke Fallon).

him and Connor would be there taking things apart'. John joked with me of how James could sometimes seem so far ahead of technological trends: 'I can remember when I started doing the lamps around 2010, I'd be there with my little Nokia, and Jimmy would say, "Look at my smart watch! *Hello: say hello to John!*"' In admiration, Ronan points out how James 'loves figuring out how things work', adding, 'He has that love of mechanisms. My wife, his daughter Sinéad, she also has that great love for logic.'

While they had previously contended with things like bad weather, there was something unique about the challenge of recent times. Ronan compares it to the big snow of 2010, which brought much of the city to a standstill:

> There was still the pride of doing it. I can remember 2010, and Jimmy would be dragging me out of the house on Stephen's Day to go to the park! When no vehicles could get to the

A lamp begins its labour in evening time, Chesterfield Avenue (Luke Fallon).

park. And you'd be walking, with the ladder, on Stephen's Day. I would say, 'Jimmy, not even the deer are out and you have us out in the snow!' But in Covid there was a very strong sense of duty to the park.

From upstairs in his home on Blackhorse Avenue, Frank Flanagan can see into the Phoenix Park, 'So even through it all, I was still there, looking into it from my window anyway,' he says. 'We do fortnightly reports, which go in to the OPW. So I still had that to do. But I can remember at the beginning, the notice on the turnstile up there saying "No Admission". From here to Cumiskey's, that was about as far as I went in the beginning.' For James, who lives in the western suburbs, it was almost therapeutic to be able to go to work, at a time when people couldn't move across the city. 'You'd have the ladder on the car, the high-vis jacket. Being waved into an empty park. Surreal is a word I'd use to describe those times. When I was going there first, there was absolutely nobody there. Only traffic passing through. But it was very strange to see it with nobody walking in it even at the beginning.'

The Phoenix Park will be a memory, for many of us, of those recent and trying years. A place where we walked the dog in brief escapism, where we took up running or jogging, or where we met friends. The increased visitor numbers of recent years are testament to that. Still, behind the walls of Áras an Uachtaráin is another reminder, with an oak tree in the commemorative garden planted by President Higgins and Sabina Higgins in March 2022, dedicated to the memory of those lost and to acknowledge the bravery of frontline workers. On that day of reflection, President Higgins spoke of how 'it is important we remember the many remarkable ways that we have come together as a people to support each other, and in particular the most vulnerable, over the course of the pandemic'.[5] When the history of that pandemic is written in an Irish context, the Phoenix Park and spaces like it will be a part of the story.

---

5 Speech by President Higgins, 20 March 2022. See https://president.ie/en/media-library/news-releases/president-and-sabina-higgins-to-hold-remembrance-ceremony-for-those-who-died-from-covid-19.

Donal Fallon Acknowledgements

First and foremost, my thanks to all in the extended Flanagan family without whom this book could not have been written. Their willingness to share stories, and to allow many family images to be reproduced here, was vital to this project succeeding. My thanks to all at Hachette Ireland who believed in this idea and who approached me with it. It is a special and unique story, a small part of the massive tapestry that makes up Dublin. I can recall visiting the Flanagan home with Ciara Doorley for the first time, and instantly knowing this was something I wanted to be associated with. Sincere thanks to Aonghus Meaney, who brought much clarity and guidance to the manuscript.

I have to acknowledge the work of Kathleen Harris in *The Irish Times*. Perhaps this book would not exist without her. In October 2022, Kathleen produced a beautiful short video and accompanying text piece for the newspaper about Frank and James. It was, as internet lingo would have it, a viral hit. There was something about the time when it was posted that no doubt played a part in its securing such a wide reach. After the harshness of 2020 and 2021, and the gradual lifting of gloom in 2022, this wholesome tale about a place many of us had fallen in love with during the pandemic really captured the attention of the public.

Part oral history, this study is indebted to the work of Kevin C. Kearns. His interview with Tom Flanagan, which first appeared in *Dublin Street Life and Lore*, was vital in telling the story of the family profession in a time before Frank and James. In 2021, Kearns was honoured with the awarding of the lord mayor's scroll from Dublin City Council. This was a fitting tribute. I hope Kevin is aware of the influence he has had on me and a generation of Dublin historians.

My thanks to Luke Fallon for taking many of the images within this work. It was a real joy to accompany him on visits to the Phoenix Park, and there is no doubt but that the black-and-white images add to the atmospheric feel of the book. Shooting anything on film is always a risk, but there was a certain magic in doing it that way, even if the weather threatened proceedings. I feel these images really capture something special.

Paul McDonnell, Margaret Gormley and John McCullen were all generous with their time and information. McCullen's first history of the Phoenix Park, telling its story up to 1880, is essential reading for those keen to know more about this extraordinary space, and I eagerly look forward to his next volume. I hope this book captures something of what Dubliners owe to McCullen. In Gormley, McDonnell and their teams, there is also a strong commitment to this beautiful space going forward. To step inside Whitefields and see operational parts of the Phoenix Park I never knew existed was an eye-opening experience.

Sincere thanks to my partner Sarah Rochford, who is a constant supporter of all I do. Thanks also to Las and Maria Fallon. The Phoenix Park is a place that recalls childhood visits with both. My deep love for the city of Dublin owes a lot to both of my parents, who filled our home with history and culture. I also owe my appreciation for labour history to Las and his pioneering work on the Dublin Fire Brigade.

Thanks to the staff of the National Library of Ireland, the National Gallery of Ireland, the Royal Irish Academy, Military Archives, Dublin City Library and Archive and other cultural institutions whose collections have added to this work. We are deeply fortunate to have such institutions in this city, with a strong sense of the importance of making archival material available to the public. The freedom to access resources like the *Dictionary of Irish Biography* and the Bureau of Military History from home has transformed historic research in Ireland.

Thanks to all colleagues in the Dublin City Council Culture Company for historic sites like 14 Henrietta Street and Richmond

Barracks: it has been a privilege to work alongside so many people who are passionate about history and heritage.

As ever, my thanks to all listeners of the 'Three Castles Burning' podcast, in particular those who have supported the podcast financially and allowed it to continue as an independent venture. The success of *Three Castles Burning: A History of Dublin in Twelve Streets*, was something that transformed my life, and introduced a whole new audience. There are many, many more episodes of the podcast to come.

Luke Fallon

Frank and James Flanagan
Acknowledgements

Our initial thanks must go to Ciara Doorley and Joanna Smyth who first suggested that there was a book in the story about the gas lamplighters of the Phoenix Park.

We thank our extended Flanagan family, especially our parents Tom and T who taught us family values, that last to this day, as well as the stories of past years.

We sincerely thank our fellow author Donal Fallon, for his sterling work and expertise in extracting the material from the past and present that went into making this book.

We have to acknowledge *The Irish Times*, who first saw the potential for a story of interest in the lamplighters, and who created the video and published the story in their newspaper.

We acknowledge with thanks the continuing assistance of the OPW in the Phoenix Park.

A necessary part of the stories of the past is the Hole in the Wall pub and its owner Martin McCaffrey. Also, a valuable contribution came from the residents of Black Horse Lane (the Laners) with whom we always identify. Finally, we salute the characters of the past who established a culture and a great tradition which we seek to uphold into the future!

Appendix

The Old Lamplighter

Helen Flanagan

In Dublin in the years long past,
Our streets and parks were lit by gas.
By lamps ornate on iron stand,
All lit by taper, wick and hand.

Lamplighters in our family tree,
Go back in time to 1870.
When Nicholas Flanagan the first of the clan,
Arrived on the scene as our future man.

In 1890 he took the job in the Park,
And brought the light to those in the dark.
To the travellers he was a welcome sight,
But to lovers, well – they rejected the light!

In 1907 Nick's son Tom was born,
A handsome chap one October morn.
A future lamplighter as time would tell,
On his orange bike with ladder and bell.

When Tom grew up, and Nick retired,
Tom looked for the job, and he was hired.
They were happy days as he did his rounds,
Meeting old friends as they walked their hounds.

As time went on and technology grew,
The lamps were fitted with clocks all new.
Each week he'd set these clocks and wind,
So all the lights were sure and timed.

Tom's fame grew for years on end,
As the friendly lamplighter with time to spend.
His happy smile known far and wide,
Til '85 when he finally retired.

Then Flanagan Brothers took on the task,
To keep the flag flying at full mast.
The next generation continues the course,
To the end of the century ... and maybe more.

Select Bibliography

Primary Sources

1901 Census, National Archives of Ireland.

1911 Census, National Archives of Ireland.

Bureau of Military History collection, courtesy of the Military Archives, Ireland Dáil Éireann/Seanad Éireann Debates – © Copyright Houses of the Oireachtas 1929; 1941; 1978.

Dublin Corporation Minute Books, Dublin City Library and Archive ESB Archives online.

Flanagan Family Materials.

Phoenix Park Conservation Reports.

President.ie – Speeches of President Michael D. Higgins.

Newspapers and Journals

Belfast News Letter

Drogheda Independent

Dublin Evening Mail

Dublin Historical Record (Journal of the Old Dublin Society)

Dublin Penny Journal

Evening Herald

Evening Press

Freeman's Journal

The Guardian

Irish Independent

Irish Mirror

The Irish Press

The Irish Times (particularly the excellent 'An Irishman's Diary')

James Joyce Quarterly

Journal of Ecology
New International
Proceedings of the Royal Irish Academy
Saothar (Journal of the Irish Labour History Society)
Sunday Independent

Books

Arnold, Dana, *Rural Urbanism: London Landscapes in the Early Nineteenth Century* (Manchester, 2005).

Bracken, Audrey and Bracken, Gregory, *Dublin Strolls: Exploring Dublin's Architectural Treasures* (Cork, 2016).

Caprani, Vincent, *A Walk Around Dublin* (Dublin, 1992).

Caprani, Vincent, *Rowdy Rhymes and Rec-im-itations: Doggerel for a Departed Dublin* (Gill Books: Dublin, 1982).

Craig, Maurice, *Dublin 1660–1850* (Dublin, 1969).

Crosbie, Paddy, *Your Dinner's Poured Out!* (Dublin, 1981).

Daly, Mary E., *Dublin: The Deposed Capital* (Cork, 2011).

de Courcy, Catherine, *Dublin Zoo: An Illustrated History* (Cork, 2009).

Dickson, David, *Dublin: The Making of a Capital City* (London, 2014.

Dickson, David, *The First Irish Cities: An Eighteenth-Century Transformation* (London, 2021).

Doyle, Roddy, *Rory and Ita* (Dublin, 2008).

Dunne, John J., *Streets Broad and Narrow* (Dublin, 1982).

Evans, Bryce, *Ireland during the Second World War: Farewell to Plato's Cave* (Manchester, 2014).

Fallon, Donal, *The Pillar: The Life and Afterlife of the Nelson Pillar* (Dublin, 2014).

Fallon, Donal, *Three Castles Burning: A History of Dublin in Twelve Streets* (Dublin, 2021).

Fujita, Motoko, *The Shadow of James Joyce: Chapelizod and Environs* (Dublin, 2011).

Galway Labour History Group, *Growing Up Poor* (Galway, 1993).

Harvey, John, *Dublin: A Study in Environment* (London, 1949).

Kavanagh, Julie, *The Irish Assassins: Conspiracy, Revenge and the Murders that Stunned an Empire* (London, 2021).

Kearns, Kevin C., *Dublin Street Life and Lore* (Dublin, 1991).

Kearns, Kevin C., *In Our Day: An Oral History of Dublin's Bygone Days* (Dublin, 2022).

Kearns, Kevin C., *Stoneybatter: Dublin's Inner Urban Village* (Dublin, 1996).

Kelleher, D.H., *The Glamour of Dublin* (Dublin, 1929).

Kenna, Shane, *The Invincibles: The Phoenix Park Assassinations and the Conspiracy that Shook an Empire* (Dublin, 2019).

Kenny, Mary (ed.), *3 Days in September: When the Pope Came to Ireland* (Dublin, 2004).

Kilfeather, Siobhán Marie, *Dublin: A Cultural History* (Oxford, 2005)

Kinsella, Thomas, *A Dublin Documentary* (Dublin, 2006).

Kinsella, Thomas, *Nightwalker and Other Poems* (Dublin, 1968).

McCullen, John A., *An Illustrated History of the Phoenix Park: Landscape and Management to 1880* (Dublin, 2009).

McDonald, Frank, *A Little History of the Future of Dublin* (Dublin, 2021).

McDonald, Frank, *The Destruction of Dublin* (Dublin, 1985).

Morash, Chris, *Dublin: A Writer's City* (Cambridge, 2023).

Moylan, Terry (ed.), *A Living Voice: The Frank Harte Song Collection* (Dublin, 2020).

Mullee, John E., *Growing Up in Dublin: Reflections from the 1950s* (Dublin, 2015).

Mulvihill, Mary, *Ingenious Ireland: A County-by-County Exploration of Irish Mysteries and Marvels* (Dublin, 2002).

Murphy, Brian, *Forgotten Patriot: Douglas Hyde and the Foundation of the Irish Presidency* (Dublin, 2016).

Neary, Bernard, *Dublin 7* (Dublin, 2016).

Nolan, Brendan, *Phoenix Park: A History and Guidebook* (Dublin, 2006).

O'Brien, J.A., *Against the Wind: Memoir of a Dissident Dubliner* (Victoria, 2013).

O'Clery, Conor, *Phrases Make History Here* (Dublin, 1987).

O'Sullivan, Charles J., *The Gasmakers: Historical Perspectives on the Irish Gas Industry* (Dublin, 1987).

O'Sullivan, Seamus, *The Lamplighter, and other poems* (Dublin, 1929).

Pakenham, Thomas and Pakenham, Valerie (eds.), *Dublin: A Traveller's Reader* (London, 2003).

Plunkett, James, *Strumpet City* (London, 1969).

Pritchett, V.S., *Dublin: A Portrait* (London, 1967).

Robinson, Mary, *Everybody Matters: A Memoir* (London, 2012).

Ryan, Michael, *My Life in the IRA* (Cork, 2018).

Sommerville-Large, Peter, *Dublin: The Fair City* (London, 1996).

von Noorden, Djinn (ed.), *Malton's Views of Dublin: The Story of a Georgian City* (Dublin, 2021).

Wills, Clair, *That Neutral Island: A History of Ireland During the Second World War* (London, 2007).

Woodward, Guy, *Culture, Northern Ireland, and the Second World War* (Oxford, 2015).

Permissions Acknowledgements

Text

Permission granted from Liberties Press for the extracts from Maurice Craig, *Dublin 1660-1860* (1969).

Permission granted from Faber and Faber Ltd. for the poem 'Beacons at Bealtaine' by Seamus Heaney, quoted in Chris Morash, *Dublin: A Writers' City* (2023).

Permission granted from Cló Iar-Chonnacht for the poem 'Fear Lasta Lampaí' by Máirtín Ó Direáin, quoted in Charles J. Sullivan, *The Gasmakers: Historical Perspectives on the Irish Gas Industry* (1987).

Permission granted from The O'Brien Press Ltd. for the extracts from *Your Dinner's Poured Out* by Paddy Crosbie (1981).

Permission granted from Paula Meehan for the poem 'The Pattern' from Paula Meehan, *The Man who was Marked by Winter* (1991).

Permission granted from The Old Dublin Society for the extract from Colum McCabe, 'History of the Town Gas Industry in Ireland 1823-1980' in *Dublin Historical Record* (Volume 45, Number 1), 28-40.

Permission granted from Martello Publishing for the extract from Frank McDonald, *A Little History of the Future of Dublin* (2021).

Permission granted from Little Brown Book Group Limited for the extract from Thomas Pakenham and Valerie Pakenham (eds), *Dublin: A Traveller's Reader* (2003). Reproduced with permission of the Licensor through PLSclear.

Permission granted from Oxford Publishing Limited for the extract from *Paul Rouse, Sport and Ireland: A History* (Oxford, 2015). Reproduced with permission of the Licensor through PLSclear.

Permission granted from Military Archives, Ireland for the extracts from the Bureau of Military History collection.

Permission granted from *The Irish Times* for the extract from Dean Ruxton, *The Irish Times*, 2 March 2018.

Permission granted from Bob Montgomery for the extract from Bob Montgomery, *The Irish International Grand Prix 1929–1931* (2019).

Permission granted from Gill Books for the extract from Vincent Caprani, *Rowdy Rhymes and Rec-im-itations: Doggerel for a Departed Dublin* (1982).

Permission granted from Houses of the Oireachtas for Ireland Dáil Éireann/ Seanad Éireann Debates – © Copyright Houses of the Oireachtas 1929; 1941; 1978.

Permission granted from Yale French Studies for the extract from Wolfgang Schievelbusch, 'The Policing of Street Lighting', Yale French Studies (Number 73, 1987), 61–71.

Every effort has been made to clear permissions for the poem 'The Lamplighter' from Seamus O'Sullivan, *The Lamplighter & Other Poems* (1929). Please contact the publisher with any queries.

Every effort has been made to clear permissions for the extract from Rebecca Boyd, 'Raiding the Vikings: How Does Ireland Consume Its Viking Heritage?' in Tom Birkett and Roderick Dale (eds), *The Vikings Reimagined: Reception, Recovery, Engagement* (Michigan, 2019), 232–49. Please contact the publisher with any queries.

Images

The author and publisher would like to thank the following for permission to use inside images in *The Lamplighters of the Phoenix Park*:

Alamy: 34, 129
Dublin City Library and Archive: ii, xxi, xxii, xxx–xxxi, 12–13, 22, 36–37, 66, 72–73, 74, 81, 108–109, 110, 133, 142–143, 170–171, 186–187, 188, 196
John Byrne: 120
John McCullen: 154
Military Archives: 30, 83
National Gallery of Ireland: 16

The images used on the following pages are reproduced courtesy of the National Library of Ireland with NLI call numbers indicated:

Page 3: DCC 70

Page 6: Pd 2087 tx[51]

Page 23: Et B412

Page 26: Et A418

Page 28: Et A417

Page 41: Lroy 2988

Page 42: Oco 197

Page 47: Lcab 8937

Page 52: Hogw 125

Page 55: Eph C421

Page 63: Indh 449

Page 79: Indh 1552

Page 80: Pd 4309 tx1[1]

Page 85: Eph F128

Page 88: Oke/32

Page 95: Pd2159 tx[16]28

Page 97: Lroy 5471

Page 98: Lroy 8910

Page 115: Oco 200

Page 117: Eas 1714

Page 122 (right): Lroy 676

Page 124: Eas 1713

Page 125: Et A423

Page 127: Pd c58

Page 131: Pd weeklyfreeman 1882 May 13[a]

Page 136: Eph F226

The author and publisher have endeavoured to contact all copyright holders. If any images or text used in this book have been reproduced without permission, we encourage owners of copyright not acknowledged to contact us at info@hbgi.ie